The
Glenstal Companion
to the
Easter Vigil

Editors Luke Macnamara OSB
Martin Browne OSB

The
Glenstal Companion
to the
Easter Vigil

DOMINICAN PUBLICATIONS

First published (2019) by
Dominican Publications
42 Parnell Square
Dublin 1

ISBN 978-1-905604-41-8

British Library Cataloguing in Publications Data.
A catalogue record for this book is available
from the British Library.

Copyright © (2019) The Authors and Dominican Publications

All rights reserved.
No part of this publication may be reproduced, stored in a retrieval system or transmitted by any means, electronic or mechanical, including photocopying, without permission in writing from the publisher.

Cover design by
David Cooke

Cover Image
Resurrection by Emmaus O'Herlihy OSB
Oil on canvas (polyptych), 2011, 244 cm *x* 360 cm

Woken to ever-lasting life, the dead corpus is bolted back to consciousness.
Atrophied limbs flush with new life. Dead, dulled flesh becomes radiant.
Christ inhales the breath of life sent by the Father while still buried in a tomb under the earth.
The wounds of torture and death remain, transformed as symbols of the self-emptying love of God that redeems all.

Printed in Ireland by
SPRINT-print, Rathcoole, Co. Dublin

Contents

Contributors   7

Introduction   9

Part I
The Easter Vigil

'Now that we have begun our Solemn Vigil...'   13
An Introduction to the Easter Vigil in the Holy Night
BRENDAN COFFEY, OSB

Part II
The Readings of the Vigil

1   What is the Beginning of Everything?   29
      First Reading • Genesis 1:1-2:2
      TERENCE CROTTY, OP

2   A Costly Sacrifice   42
      Second Reading • Genesis 22:1-18
      LUKE MACNAMARA, OSB

3   Crossing the Red Sea   56
      Third Reading • Exodus 14:15-15:1
      FRANCIS COUSINS

4	Discovering God in the Desert *Fourth Reading • Isaiah 54:5-14* JESSIE ROGERS	71
5	The Fountain and the Banquet *Fifth Reading • Isaiah 55:1-11* COLUMBA McCANN, OSB	85
6	Return to the Fountain of Wisdom *Sixth Reading • Baruch 3:9-15, 32-4:4* SUSAN DOCHERTY	99
7	Water, Heart and Spirit *Seventh Reading • Ezekiel 36:16-28* MARTIN BROWNE, OSB	113
8	Baptised into Christ Jesus – Alive for God *Eighth Reading • Romans 6:3-11* MARY T. O'BRIEN, PBVM	127
9	Dawning *Gospel Year A • Matthew 28:1-10* CÉLINE MANGAN, OP	138
10	The Open Tomb and the Well-Spring of Life *Gospel Year B • Mark 16:1-7* LUKE MACNAMARA, OSB	148
11	Witnesses of the Resurrection *Gospel Year C • Luke 24:1-12* THOMAS ESPOSITO, O CIST	161

Contributors

Brendan Coffey, O.S.B., has been Abbot of Glenstal since 2016. He pursued postgraduate studies in Liturgy at the Institute of Pastoral Liturgy in Padua and Catholic University in Washington DC. He is a member of the Council for Liturgy of the Irish Catholic Bishops' Conference.

Terence Crotty, O.P., is Master of Students for the Irish Province. He holds a doctorate in Sacred Scripture from the University of Fribourg.

Luke Macnamara, O.S.B., is a monk of Glenstal Abbey and lecturer in Sacred Scripture at St Patrick's College, Maynooth. He holds a doctorate in Sacred Scripture from the Pontifical Biblical Institute in Rome.

Francis Cousins lectures in Religious Education at St Angela's College, Sligo. Having completed a Masters in Biblical Theology, he is in the final year of the doctorate programme in Scripture at Durham University.

Jessie Rogers lectures in Sacred Scripture at St Patrick's College, Maynooth. She holds a doctorate in Scripture from the University of Stellenbosch.

Columba McCann, O.S.B., is a monk of Glenstal Abbey, where he currently serves as Novice Master and Oblate Director. He holds a licence in Sacred Liturgy from the Pontifical Liturgical Institute in Rome. He is an organist and recitalist and a composer of liturgical music.

Susan Docherty is Professor of New Testament and Early Judaism and Head of Theology at Newman University, Birmingham. She holds a doctorate from the University of Manchester.

Martin Browne, O.S.B., is a monk of Glenstal Abbey and former Headmaster of the abbey school. Among other responsibilities he currently serves as liturgical Master of Ceremonies in the abbey.

Mary T. O'Brien, P.B.V.M., is a lecturer in Biblical Studies at Mary Immaculate College, Limerick. She holds a doctorate from the University of Limerick.

Céline Mangan, O.P., was formerly Associate Professor in the Milltown Institute in Dublin. She holds a licence in Sacred Scripture from the Pontifical Biblical Institute in Rome.

Thomas Esposito, O.Cist., is a monk of the Abbey of Our Lady of Dallas, Texas, and Assistant Professor of Theology at Constantin College, University of Dallas. He holds a doctorate in Sacred Scripture from the Pontifical Biblical Institute in Rome.

Introduction

From earliest times, the Church has celebrated Easter, the feast of feasts, by means of a night vigil. The Easter Vigil is rightly known as the 'mother of all holy vigils'. As the Church's instruction on the celebration of Easter puts it: 'The Resurrection of Christ is the foundation of our faith and hope, and through Baptism and Confirmation, we are inserted into the Paschal Mystery of Christ, dying, buried, and raised with him, and with him, we shall also reign. The full meaning of Vigil is a waiting for the coming of the Lord.'

The expectant waiting of the Easter Vigil is expressed in an extended Liturgy of the Word, as the assembly basks in the light of the Paschal Candle. However, the Vigil's series of Old Testament readings is abbreviated in many worshipping communities, often extremely so. If the Vigil also happens to be scheduled for early in the evening, before the sun has set, there is little outward difference between the Easter Vigil and any other Saturday evening Mass. This is far from what is envisaged by the liturgy itself. The very nature of a vigil implies that it be a somewhat prolonged celebration.

One of the reasons why some communities might omit one or more readings is that they can sometimes seem inaccessible or irrelevant to the feast being celebrated. Some of them may seem cruel or even barbaric. Even when most or all of the readings are proclaimed during the Vigil, it is not easy to draw from them all in the homily; and so the reason for their inclusion may not be clear. Yet the Easter Vigil readings were all chosen because of the light they shed on the central reality of the Christian faith – the Paschal Mystery of Jesus Christ. Spending some time and effort on deepening our encounter with God's Word in these texts will surely enrich our celebration of the Vigil.

This collection has its origins in a series of Sunday afternoon talks in Glenstal Abbey during Lent 2018. There are more readings in the Easter Vigil than Sundays in Lent, and so the idea was born of inviting further contributions and producing a collection that covers the seven Old Testament readings, the Epistle, and the Gospel readings for Years A, B and C. Some of the contributors are academic Scripture scholars while others have liturgical or more general theological interests. This means that each chapter has a distinctive approach and style. Each contributor was asked to examine a single Vigil reading, in its liturgical context, so as to provide real and substantial information and nourishment in an attractive and accessible way.

As the title states, this book is intended to be a companion to the Easter Vigil. It can never take the place of the experience of actually hearing the readings proclaimed in the liturgical assembly. But it can help to enrich that experience. Whether it is used for private reflection and prayer by an individual, as an aid to preparation by a reader or preacher, or in Scripture or liturgy groups, the aim of the book is simply to enable readers to enter more deeply into the readings of the Easter Vigil. Our hope is that it will be a rich resource, year after year, for any Christian who wishes to read, study and pray with the full selection of Scripture provided by the Church for this 'truly blessed night, when things of heaven are wed to those of earth'.

Luke Macnamara OSB
Martin Browne OSB   Glenstal Abbey

PART ONE

The Easter Vigil

'Now that we have begun our Solemn Vigil...'

An Introduction to the Easter Vigil in the Holy Night

BRENDAN COFFEY, O.S.B.

Background

The Easter Vigil did not come into existence on 9 February 1951 when Pope Pius XII allowed its celebration *ad experimentum* during the night for the first time in many centuries.[1] The Easter Vigil is, in fact, the oldest of the Triduum ceremonies, being celebrated from the early centuries. Most scholars today believe that the original practice was to have onlóy one great celebration at Easter which encompassed the Passion, death and Resurrection of the Lord.[2] This was later to become three separate liturgies; the Mass of the Lord's Supper; the Passion of the Lord and the Easter Vigil. The Easter Vigil occupied the entire night of Holy Saturday in the third and fourth centuries. At this period in history no further liturgy was celebrated on Easter Day. The earliest surviving copy of the Easter Vigil liturgy is an Armenian Easter Vigil in Jerusalem which dates from the fifth century.[3] Once we get to the sixth century the

---

1. Adolf Adam, *The Liturgical Year: Its History and Its Meaning after the Reform of the Liturgy* (Collegeville, MN: Liturgical Press, 1992), 64.
2. Ibid., 63.
3. Charles Renoux, ed., *Le lectionnaire de Jérusalem en Arménie* (Turnhout: Brepols, 1989).

Vigil had already been shortened and was ending before midnight, so a separate Mass had appeared for Easter Sunday. By the eighth century it was permissible, though not obligatory, to begin the Vigil once the first star had appeared in the night sky. When we move on to the ninth century we find things had slipped further and it was permitted to begin the Vigil after the office of None (about 3.00 pm).[4]

Skipping on several more centuries, we find that by the fourteenth century church law allowed None to be prayed in the morning hours if desired and so the Vigil could also be celebrated on the morning of Holy Saturday. The Missal of Pius V, the Missal of Trent (1570), made this arrangement not only possible but obligatory and so it was no longer permitted to have the Easter Vigil in the afternoon or evening.

So we had an incongruous situation where the Easter Candle was being lit and the *Lumen Christi* sung while the sun was shining brightly into the church, the Resurrection was proclaimed and yet the people knew full well that their Triduum fast did not end until after noon on Holy Saturday as this was the day in which Christ lay in the tomb.

This was obviously a most bizarre situation and anyone who knew anything at all about the history of the liturgy could easily see that this made no sense whatsoever. The experiment of Pius XII in 1951 became the norm in 1955 and the Church has celebrated the Easter Vigil after dark on Holy Saturday evening since that time. In 1955, the Holy See offered the following reasons for its radical reform of the Easter Vigil and Holy Week ceremonies:

> In the middle ages various causes conspired to bring them forward earlier and earlier into the day, so that eventually they became morning functions, impairing the earlier har-

---

4. Adam, *The Liturgical Year*, 76.

mony with the accounts given in the Gospel narratives. This disharmony was most glaring on the Saturday, which became liturgically the day of Resurrection instead of that day's eve, and, liturgically again, from a day of darkest mourning became a day of light and gladness.[5]

The 1951 reintroduction of the Vigil was important for another reason. It was the first liturgy in hundreds of years to assign an active role to the faithful. The structure of the Vigil has changed remarkably little from early times, but obviously, as with everything else, there have been some changes and a certain amount of evolution. So let's begin by having a look at some of these changes and the reasons for them.

Structure

There are four parts to the Easter Vigil: the Liturgy of Light; the Liturgy of the Word; the Liturgy of Baptism; and the Liturgy of the Eucharist. Oddly enough, it is the Liturgy of Light which has seen most change and development.

The old Roman liturgy didn't have a blessing for the Easter Fire. This blessing is of Frankish origin and it was intended to displace the spring fires lit by pagans in honour of Wotan, or Odin as he is sometimes called, the king of the gods.[6] The Romans did have a fire, in fact they had several fires. In the eighth century the Romans lit many fires around the city on Holy Thursday after the chrism was consecrated and these were kept going until Holy Saturday night and were used to light the candles of the faithful for the Vigil. The commission for the revision of the Easter Vigil after Vatican II actually contemplated getting rid of the fire altogether but decided against it because it was much loved by the people.

5. Ibid., 77.
6. Ibid., 76.

The Easter Candle originated with the widespread custom in Rome and elsewhere of lighting up Easter night with candles, symbolising Christ who has been raised from the night of death. Originally, according to Adolf Adam in his study of the liturgical year, there appear to have been two Easter candles, each about the size of a person, but this was relatively quickly reduced to one and the Gallic liturgy then added a special blessing and the further symbols of the Cross, alpha and omega and the date.[7] The *Exsultet* is also of Gallic origin and dates probably from the seventh century. It first appears in the *Missale Gothicum* of the seventh century and in the *Bobbio Missal* of the late seventh century and so there is an interesting Irish connection there.

In the Christian East there is no direct parallel with the Paschal Candle but the priest or presiding bishop does carry a *paschal trikirion* or triple candle in his hand. The people carry candles just as we do. So the people's lighted candles came first and the Paschal Candle later. Not what one might expect perhaps? In the Ambrosian Rite there is a Paschal Candle but it doesn't carry the engravings of Cross, date, *etc*. It is a large plain candle, remaining faithful to the older tradition. In the middle ages, the Paschal Candle of Salisbury Cathedral was said to have been 36 feet tall. That is not as unusual as it may seem, because by the Middle Ages the Paschal Candle had become so large it was no longer carried in procession and small candles arranged in a triangle had replaced it for the purposes of the procession.[8]

The five grains of incense which are inserted into the candle with pins in memory of the five wounds of Christ possibly derive from a medieval misunderstanding.[9] In the Gelasian Sacramen-

---

7. Ibid., 78.
8. Kenneth W. Stevenson, *Worship: Wonderful and Sacred Mystery* (Washington, DC: Pastoral Press, 1992), 199.
9. Paul Turner, *Glory in the Cross: Holy Week the Third Edition of the Roman Missal* (Collegeville, MN: Liturgical Press, 2011), 122.

tary (the sacramentary of the parish liturgy of Rome), there was a prayer called *Benedictio super incensum* which means 'Blessing on the lighted candle' but was possibly misunderstood to mean 'Blessing on the incense' and so grains of incense were placed into the candle – a rather peculiar action. Over time, meaning is attached to liturgical action and so here the incense came to represent the five wounds of Christ and the candle bears the wounds as does the body of the risen Lord.

Moving to the Liturgy of the Word, this is what makes the Vigil a vigil. Paul Turner in his 2011 study of Holy Week notes in relation to the Vigil that 'the length of the service is one of its primary symbols'.[10] From the earliest of times the long vigil in the night was punctuated by readings, hymns, psalms and prayers. The only thing that has changed here is the number and choice of readings. The present selection of readings has been painstakingly put together to reflect the mystery of salvation which we celebrate. The *Gloria* now marks the transition from the Old to New Testaments. In the past it has been in different locations, including at the end of the rite of Baptism as a post-baptismal hymn of praise.[11] The Alleluia returns with great solemnity before the Gospel, after being absent for the duration of Lent.

Baptism and the celebration of the sacraments of initiation on this holy night are likewise attested to from earliest times in both the East and the West; even Egeria of the late fourth century mentions them.[12] There are no shortage of homilies from those early centuries about Baptism and the Easter Mystery. The Church has always looked upon the fire and flame as symbolising Christ's victory over death and water and the font as the sign of our participation in that victory. We will return to the symbolic aspects

10. Turner, *Glory in the Cross*, 131.
11. Ibid., 141.
12. Ibid., 145.

of this later. The prayer for the blessing of the water imitates the structure of the Eucharistic Prayer. It has an *anamnesis* (remembering), recalling the institution of Baptism, and an *epiclesis*, invoking of the Holy Spirit on the waters. This structure is more obvious in the prayer of blessing used if there are candidates for Baptism. If someone is to be baptised, the Paschal Candle is dipped into the waters of the font as part of the blessing. This practice goes back, once again, to the Gelasian Sacramentary and the eighth century. We then renew our baptismal promises and are sprinkled with the Easter water.[13]

The Vigil climaxes in a joyous celebration of the Eucharist. The risen Lord invites all to participate in the new life he brings by sharing the feast which he has prepared. We thus look forward to the great messianic feast of the kingdom of God when the redeemed from every time and place 'will come from east and west, and from north and south, and sit at table in the kingdom of God'. (Luke 13:29) The Vigil thus celebrates what God has done, is doing, and will do.

When?

The structure of the Easter Vigil may be familiar to many, but what does it all mean? Why do we continue with this celebration and the use of these symbols? And what do they have to say to us today? What follows are some reflections on the main symbols of the Easter Vigil.

Firstly, I think it is very important to realise that nature herself is proclaiming the Resurrection all around us at Easter. The celebration of Easter has long been linked to the spring equinox. This is a moment of perfect balance between light and darkness and this is our first great symbol in the Easter Vigil – light and darkness.

---

13. Ibid., 150.

An Introduction to the Easter Vigil

The Council of Nicaea (325 CE) set the date of Easter as the Sunday following the paschal full moon, which is the full moon that falls on or after the vernal (spring) equinox. An equinox occurs twice a year when the tilt of the Earth's axis is inclined neither away from nor towards the sun, the centre of the sun being in the same plane as the earth's equator; a day of perfect balance.

We know that Easter must always occur on a Sunday, because Sunday was the day of Christ's Resurrection. But what is the significance of the paschal full moon? Put simply, that was how the date of Passover was calculated in the Jewish calendar and the Last Supper occurred on or near the Passover. Therefore, Easter was the Sunday after Passover.

It would be easy to think that this is a very complicated way of doing something very simple. Why go to all of that trouble? Why not just fix a date and end all this confusion? It would mean that planning the year would be so much easier as everything could be standardised. For a Christian there are other considerations because Easter follows the full moon for its symbolic value; the symbolism of light and darkness, the foundational symbol on which the Easter Vigil is built.

What we do in our Easter Vigil reflects almost exactly what the world of nature is doing around us. Today with all our electric and artificial lighting we have lost touch with some things in the natural world. We no longer experience the wonder of the full moon on a clear night where the sun shines from morning till evening and then the full moon shines from evening till morning. It is a day without night. Much as Christmas is tied to the winter solstice – the moment in the year when the light begins to conquer the darkness – Easter is tied to the full moon of the spring equinox, the day without night. The fire and candles of the Easter Vigil take up this theme which is already present in nature itself and they turn the darkness of night into endless day. Just as

Good Friday became a day of darkness when the sun disappeared from the sky, Easter Sunday is a day without night, filled with the light of the Risen One.

Light and Fire

As we move into the Liturgy of the Word this same great symbol of light and darkness returns as the very first reading we hear is the story of creation. In the beginning there was darkness over the deep and God's Spirit hovered over the water. We start at the beginning because God was before the beginning. When God spoke, there was light. The Word of God brings light into the darkness of the deep. It brings light into the darkness of the world and it brings light into the darkness of my own life. The Word is Christ and Christ himself brings light. The spoken word is a powerful tool. It can bring light into the deep darkness of another human being if the word I speak is from Christ. It can also bring great harm if my spoken word comes from my own darkness, my jealousy, my insecurity or my selfishness. If the Word of God is alive within me then that is what people will hear from me when I speak. In the beginning is freedom. Hence it is good to be a human person.

God is busy in this story of creation. He goes on to create heaven and earth, he divides the waters from the dry land, creates the vegetation and plants. He places lights in the heavens and divides night from day. He creates the fish of the sea, the birds of the air and the animals on the earth. He saw that all of this was good.

Then God reaches the climax of his creation, man and woman. We are God's work of art and if only we could believe this we would have restored the lost paradise of the Garden of Eden. It can be so easy for a Christian to believe in the sanctity of human life in a general sense and so difficult to believe that the people I have to live with are actually temples of the Holy Spirit and that in my daily dealings with them I worship the Lord and Master of my life. All of this and much, much more is contained in our first symbol.

Closely related to the symbol of light is the instrument of that light – fire. Fire is absolutely fascinating. You can sit and watch a fire for ages, with its different warm colours, its glow, its heat and the way it dances. It is truly captivating. Fire is also powerful and we respect it. You do not put your hand into the fire if you know what's good for you. Fire has the power to consume everything. It isn't difficult to understand why almost every religion that has ever been, uses fire as a symbol for God.

Fire is almost unique in its properties. It can be divided as many times as you wish and still loses nothing of its original brightness. This is exactly what we do in our Vigil. The fire is taken from the blessed Easter fire and lights the Paschal Candle. The fire from the Paschal Candle in turn lights our individual candles. Each flame burns brightly and the flame of the Paschal Candle does not diminish. It is hard to think of a more appropriate symbol for the Resurrection.

After the *lucernarium*, the liturgy of light, and the singing of the *Exsultet*, we begin the Liturgy of the Word. In listening to these readings of the Vigil we hear not only the story of the relationship between God and humanity but also the story of our own individual relationships with God and our relationships with one another.

Before the liturgical reform of Vatican II there were twelve Old Testament readings and two from the New Testament. The New Testament readings have been retained. The number of Old Testament readings has been fixed at seven, of which we must choose at least three. The Church wishes to offer us an overview of salvation history, starting with creation, passing through God's choice of Israel to be his very own people, their subsequent liberation from slavery in Egypt and the testimony of the prophets down the ages.

Liturgical tradition looks upon all of these readings as prophecies. Suffice it to say that on this night the Church in the Liturgy of the Word says who she is. We say who we are as a people and that takes some time. We do this by telling our story, the story of our dealings with God and his dealings with us.

What we are grappling with is the mystery of God, the *mysterium tremendum*, as it is called. We have great difficulty understanding God, finding words to describe God and that is why symbols are so important in the Vigil.

Water and Womb

The liturgical celebration of the Easter Vigil makes use of many symbols, but it sets before us two great symbols. First, there is the fire that becomes light, examined, above and, secondly, there is the great symbol of water. This water recalls the waters of the Red Sea, the mystery of the Cross. Here, on this holy night, it is presented to us as life-giving spring water, living water. It becomes the image of the sacrament of Baptism in which we become sharers in the death and Resurrection of Jesus Christ. Just as with the symbol of light and darkness so too with the symbol of water, the Liturgy of the Word takes up the theme.

The reading from the book of Exodus is appropriate for this holy night; the story of the crossing of the Red Sea. We have the people of Israel fleeing for their lives with the Egyptians in hot pursuit. The waters part to left and to right and the people of Israel go safely through these waters. The Egyptians, however, are not so lucky. What happens is an obvious metaphor for Baptism. In these waters I am given the opportunity to free myself from all my demons, the Egyptians of the story, who lurk in the shadows and dog my heels. The waters of the Red Sea and the living waters of Baptism allow me to share in the Resurrection.

The Church has long regarded the font of Baptism and its waters as her womb. The font holds the waters of life, the waters of new birth. The inscription in the baptistery of St John Lateran, the Cathedral Church of the city of Rome and one of the oldest sites of Christian worship, says: 'At this font, the Church, our mother, gives birth from her virginal womb to the children she conceived by the power of the Holy Spirit.' The baptismal font, in the language of the early Church, is the Divine Womb whence we receive second birth as children of God.

The Lord's Day

What do these symbols have to say to us in our Christian lives? Easter has turned our daily lives upside-down. We recall that the Sabbath is the seventh day of the week, the end of the week. After six days in which we in some sense participate in God's work of creation, the Sabbath is the day of rest. It is also the day Christ lay buried in the tomb, his day of rest. But something quite unexpected happened among the early Christians: the place of the Sabbath, Saturday, the seventh day, was taken by the first day, Sunday, the beginning of the week.

As the day of the liturgical assembly, Sunday is the day for encounter with God through Jesus Christ. This is a new structure for the week. Something very significant has happened here and time has been disrupted. Our week sets out from the first day as the day of encounter with the Risen Lord. This encounter happens afresh at every celebration of the Eucharist, when the Lord enters anew into the midst of his disciples and gives himself to them, allows himself, so to speak, to be touched by them as he was by Thomas, and sits down at table with them as with the disciples on the road to Emmaus. This change is utterly extraordinary, considering that the Sabbath is so profoundly rooted in the Old Testament.

The first day, according to the Genesis account, is the day on which creation begins. Now it is the day of creation in a new way, it has become the day of the new creation. Jesus is risen and dies no more. Tertullian, a Christian writer of the third century writing on the subject of Christ's Resurrection and our resurrection says: 'Rest assured, flesh and blood, through Christ you have gained your place in heaven and in the Kingdom of God.'[14] Easter Day ushers in a new creation. That is precisely why the Church starts the liturgy on this day with the old creation, so that we can learn to understand the new one correctly and in the light of the old.

What does this mean? It means that life is stronger than death. Good is stronger than evil. Love is stronger than hate. Truth is stronger than lies. To quote Pope Benedict XVI:

> The darkness of the previous days is driven away the moment Jesus rises from the grave and himself becomes God's pure light. But this applies not only to him, not only to the darkness of those days. With the Resurrection of Jesus, light itself is created anew. He draws all of us after him into the new light of the Resurrection and he conquers all darkness. He is God's new day.[15]

The symbols of the Vigil allow us to explore these mysteries in our own lives.

On Easter night, the night of the new creation, the Church presents the mystery of light using the Paschal Candle. This is a light that lives by giving of itself. The candle shines inasmuch as it is burnt up. It gives light, inasmuch as it gives itself. The liturgy tells us here that in the paschal mystery it is Christ who gives himself to bestow the great light. Here too the mystery of Christ is made visible. Christ, the light, is fire and flame, burning up evil and so reshaping both the world and ourselves.

---

14. Patrick J. Fletcher, *Resurrection Realism: Ratzinger the Augustinian* (Eugene, OR: Cascade Books, 2014), 231.
15. Easter homily of Pope Benedict XVI, 7 April 2012.

Finally, the great hymn of the *Exsultet*, which the deacon sings at the beginning of the Easter liturgy, points us to another aspect of the candle. It reminds us that the candle has its origin in the work of bees. So the whole of creation plays its part. In the candle, creation itself becomes the bearer of the light. The bees are a living community and the living community of believers in the Church in some way resembles the activity of bees. We build up the community of light. So the candle serves as a summons to us to become involved in the community of the Church, whose purpose is to let the light of Christ shine upon the world.

In the pages of this book the readings of the Great Vigil are explored and revealed. We must always remember, however, that these readings exist in the context of this Vigil and also reveal and are themselves revealed in its celebration.

PART TWO

The Readings of the Vigil

1

What is the Beginning of Everything?

First Reading • Genesis 1:1–2:2

TERENCE CROTTY, O.P.

Introduction

In the book of Daniel the story is told of the three young men thrown into the fire by the evil king Nebuchadnezzar because of their fidelity to the God of Israel. The king looks into the furnace and sees four men, not burning but walking around and praising God. The fourth young man, the king gasps, 'looks like a son of the gods!' And they sing the song, 'O all you works of the Lord, O bless the Lord, to him be highest glory and praise for ever', and continue on through all creation: the angelic hosts, the sun and moon, showers and rain, snow and wind, all the way down to the human race and to Israel, all are called to bless the Lord.

This great canticle, recited each Sunday morning in the Church's Liturgy of the Hours, is only one of many praises of God and his creation which are found in the Scriptures. Jesus himself, when teaching about the love of God the Father, points to the wonder of creation: 'Consider the lilies of the fields; they never have to work or spin; yet I assure you that not even Solomon in all his glory was clothed like one of these.'(Matt 6:28-29) The wonder of creation is a stream bubbling through the sacred text.

The first chapter of Genesis, which we hear proclaimed at the Easter Vigil, is exactly the same – praise of God for the wonders of creation. It has often been reduced by readers and interpreters to a materialist, blow by blow, failed and outdated pseudo-scientific account of the origins of the universe. How unfortunate! It is not a historical account, but rather a polyvalent, multi-voiced account of the glory of God as Creator. It speaks of a universe that is created, that is ordered, and that is good, which God creates effortlessly and with infinite and ineffable majesty.

This is more important to know than any attempt at dating. Were I left with a choice between the truth that this chapter teaches me and the truth that a book like *A Brief History of Time* teaches me, with all due respect, the truth I read in Genesis 1 is more essential to me, though the two are, of course, complementary.

That the universe is a mystery that in no sense explains itself – *i.e.*, that it is created from without – is a given. Since the Enlightenment human beings have felt a pressing need to justify this. It is obvious that we run out of explanatory power quite quickly when observing the world. Not only that the world exists, but that it is not simply stones but has living things in it too; and not simply living things, but procreative living things that increase and multiply; and not simply living things, but thinking beings with discursive thought; and not simply that, but that the world is good and beautiful for these thinking beings to observe and to love. The English scientist John Polkinghorne writes about the success of science in modern times and reminds his readers that this success

---

> What is all this juice and all this joy?
>   A strain of the earth's sweet being in the beginning
> In Eden garden. – Have, get, before it cloy,
>   Before it cloud, Christ, lord, and sour with sinning,
> Innocent mind and Mayday in girl and boy,
>   Most, O maid's child, thy choice and worthy the winning.
>
>   GERARD MANLEY HOPKINS, *Spring*

has been purchased by the modesty of its explanatory ambition. It does not attempt to ask and answer every question that one might legitimately raise. Instead it confines itself to investigating natural processes and attending to the question of how things happened. Other questions, such as those relating to meaning and purpose, are deliberately bracketed out.[1]

Christians don't feel the need to be modest in our explanatory ambitions or to bracket out questions of meaning, because the evidence is all around us: 'In the beginning God created the heavens and the earth'. (Gen 1:1-2)

In the Beginning, God Created ... a Temple

God creates from nothing. The Hebrew word used here for his work is *bara*, an uncommon word quite different from the word which will be used in chapter 2 for the work of a craftsman moulding Adam from the dust, or the usual Hebrew word *asah*, to 'make'. Of course, when he creates, God is doing something unlike anything he will do again. He is making nothing to be something, calling into being out of nothingness. 'And the Spirit of God was moving over the face of the waters.' (1:2) The constructive force of creation is God himself and the Spirit who creates is the Spirit who sanctifies – creation and sanctification occur in the one movement. In Exodus 31:3, the Spirit of God will re-appear for the first time in the Bible, but this time for the furnishing of the Temple: 'See, I have called by name Bezalel the son of Uri, son of Hur, of the tribe of Judah: and I have filled him with the Spirit of God, with ability and intelligence, with knowledge and

---

1. John Polkinghorne, 'The Universe as Creation,' in *God and World: Theology of Creation from Scientific and Ecumenical Standpoints*, editors. Tomasz Trafny and Armand Puig I Tàrrech (Rome: Libreria Editrice Vaticana, 2011), 33.

all craftsmanship.' (Exod 31:2-3) The craftsman creates, and the Spirit sanctifies in one movement.

Creation in Genesis 1 takes seven days, with God resting like an observant Jew on the seventh. One scholar has commented: 'The seven days represent the liturgical week, the day beginning in the evening, and the week crowned by Sabbath. Sabbath was instituted at Sinai (Exod 20:8-11) though anticipated in observance at an earlier stage in the wilderness. (Exod 16:22-30) That it also crowns the work of construction of the wilderness sanctuary (Exod 31:12-17) is one of several indications of parallelism between world-building and sanctuary-building. The point is being made that Sabbath is rooted in the created order of things.'[2]

Like the Temple as seen by the Prophet Ezekiel (chapter 40), the temple of creation is full of numbers. Seven times God sees and seven times we are told 'and so it was'. Seven times God creates, ten times 'according to its kind/kinds'. Five times God 'names' things. Five times he separates. The author has it all planned out, and the order of his own writing reflects the perfect order that he sees in the divine work of creation.

The then Cardinal Joseph Ratzinger is among many who have seen in this a link also to the Ten Commandments, the same God who creates gives the Law on Sinai – each in perfect order, each in perfect goodness, each in divine wisdom. The words 'God said' appear ten times in the creation account. In this way the creation narrative anticipates the Ten Commandments. This makes us realize that these Ten Commandments are, as it were, an echo of the creation. They are not arbitrary inventions for the purpose of erecting barriers to human freedom but signs pointing to the spirit, the language, and the meaning of creation. They are a translation of the language of the universe, a translation

---

2. Joseph Blenkinsopp, *The Pentateuch: An Introduction to the First Five Books of the Bible* (New York: Doubleday, 1992), 61-63.

of God's logic, which constructed the universe.³ And we might add the converse. This means that creation is as religious as the commandments. It is oriented towards God. The Spirit hovering on the waters, the numerical ordering of the account, the almost symphonic repetition of evening and morning, and the affirmation of the goodness of what is created, the lights in the vault of heaven, 'for signs and for seasons and for days and years', and finally and most obviously, the working week of six days that comes to rest in God, all point to a creation which is directed towards worship and rest in God. God himself rests (2:2), not because he is tired but like a god resting in his Temple.

> All the juxtapositions of the liturgy call us to trust in the biblical pattern, reinterpreting our world from and living out of this: God is the one who brings something out of nothing, life out of death, the new out of the old.
>
> GORDON LATHROP, *Holy Things*

In the chapters which mirror this at the end of the Bible, in Revelation, we read of 'new heavens and a new earth', constructed exactly as a Temple, where God lives among his people, so that 'he will dwell with them, and they shall be his people, and God himself will be with them'. (Rev 21:3) So, creation begins and will end as a Temple in which God dwells among his people. The many temples in the meantime are replacements for what should be and will be a universal phenomenon. As always, the key that turns this lock is Jesus himself. It is said of him after he promised to destroy 'this temple and in three days build it up' that, 'he spoke of the temple of his body. When therefore he was raised from the dead, his disciples remembered that he had said this; and they believed the Scripture and the word which Jesus had spoken'. (John 2:21-22)

---

3. Joseph Ratzinger, *In the Beginning* (London: T&T Clark, 1995), 26.

Creation at Easter

Writing towards the middle of the second century, Melito of Sardis described Christ as

> the Passover of our salvation. This is the one who patiently endured many things in many people: This is the one who was murdered in Abel, and bound as a sacrifice in Isaac, and exiled in Jacob, and sold in Joseph, and exposed in Moses, and sacrificed in the lamb, and hunted down in David, and dishonoured in the prophets.[4]

What Bishop Melito is saying is that the story of the Old Testament is the story of Christ – an instinct present in Christians since the day of Pentecost. He is expounding here on the theme that he has first stated:

> Therefore, understand this, O beloved: The mystery of the Passover is new and old, eternal and temporal, corruptible and incorruptible, mortal and immortal in this fashion. It is old insofar as it concerns the law, but new insofar as it concerns the Gospel; temporal insofar as it concerns the type, eternal because of grace. …The law is old, but the Gospel is new; the type was for a time, but grace is forever.[5]

So too, therefore, the opening lines of the book of Genesis are the story of Christ, about whom the Evangelist said, 'all things were made through him, and without him was not anything made that was made'. (John 1:3-5) God creates by a Word: 'Let there be light', he says, 'and there was light!' And of that Word it will be said, 'the Word became flesh and dwelt among us, full of grace and truth', as the man Jesus Christ. (John 1:14) In the shining of

---

4. Melito of Sardis, *Peri Pascha*, 69. Online at http://www.kerux.com/doc/0401A1.asp.
5. *Peri Pascha*, 2-4.

light out of darkness in the act of creation, Jesus was the light. And so Genesis 1 should be seen both in terms of the law and in terms of the Gospel, in terms of creation and in terms of Christ. It is for this reason that it is the first reading in the Easter Vigil, not because it speaks of an act of creation which is past, but because it speaks of a Word and a light and a beginning who are, each of them – Word, light, and beginning – the person of Jesus Christ, about whom the Easter Vigil turns. St Athanasius writes:

> As we proceed in our exposition of [the Incarnation of the Word], we must first speak about the creation of the universe and its creator, God, so that in this way we may consider as fitting that its renewal was effected by the Word who created it in the beginning.[6]

In What Beginning?

The Hebrew word *rôshît*, 'beginning', is related to the word *rôsh*,[7] meaning 'head', so that head and beginning are related. They are related in English too when we speak of the head of a river or the heading of a page. St Paul, writing in his Letter to the Colossians, speaks of Christ as, 'the head of the body, the church; he is the beginning, the first-born from the dead, that in everything he might be pre-eminent'. (Col 1:18) Paul therefore throws a rope between Genesis 1 and the Resurrection of Christ. 'He is the beginning, the first-born from the dead.' And so the presence of this reading in the Easter Vigil liturgy begins to make perfect sense.

We should not forget the earlier lines of this hymn of Christ in the opening chapter of Colossians, with its own echoes of the light and darkness of the creation story, 'giving thanks to the Fa-

---

6. Athanasius, *On the Incarnation* 1 (ACCS 1: xlviii).
7. Having an uncanny similarity to the Irish word *Ros*, meaning a 'headland'. See Niall Ó Dónaill, ed., *Foclóir Gaeilge-Béarla*, (Dublin: Oifig an tSoláthair, 1977), 1011.

ther, who has qualified us to share in the inheritance of the saints in light. He has delivered us from the dominion of darkness and transferred us to the kingdom of his beloved Son, in whom we have redemption, the forgiveness of sins.' (Col 1:12-14) Russel Reno comments:

> Paul evokes the division of light and darkness on the first day of creation, ... [T]he Father pries the faithful out of the dominion of darkness and delivers them to their inheritance of light. (Col 1:12-13) Paul is not simply providing a symbolic, poetic use of the images of light and darkness. This passage from Colossians functions as an interpretation of Genesis 1. In Christ, Paul writes, 'all things were created in heaven and on earth, visible and invisible, whether thrones or dominions or principalities or authorities – all things were created through him and for him'. (1:16) The crucified Christ is 'the mystery hidden for ages and generations.' (1:26) Therefore, once the truth of Christ is made manifest, all things – especially the source and origin and purpose of all things – become clear.[8]

There is within the 'beginning' mentioned in the opening words of the Bible another beginning, more primordial than the beginning of the world. Because St John the Evangelist, famously re-using this passage, tells us that 'in the beginning was the Word'. (John 1:1), the Fathers of the Church saw a trinitarian stamp on this passage in Genesis – God the Father as Creator, the Spirit hovering over the face of the waters, and the Beginning, who is Christ. When Jesus is asked about his identity, he responds, as we read in the Gospel according to John: 'The beginning, who also

---

8. Russell Reno, 'Beginning with the Ending,' in *Genesis and Christian Theology*, eds. N. MacDonald, M. W. Elliott and G. Macaskill (Grand Rapids: Eerdmans, 2012), 27.

speaks unto you.' (John 8:25)

When he reads this verse, 'In the beginning, God created the heavens and the earth', the second-century Father of the Church, Origen, writes: 'Scripture is not speaking here of any temporal beginning, but it says that the heavens and the earth and all things that were made were made "in the beginning," that is, in the Saviour.'[9]

When proclaimed during the Easter Vigil, this reading speaks precisely of the ultimate new creation where, out of the nothingness and the formless void of death, Christ rises. There is a beginning. Something new has been made, in which the one action of God, Father, Son, and Spirit, has created what was never seen before. That first Easter morning saw the dawn of a new hope for humanity: 'Blessed be the God and Father of our Lord Jesus Christ! By his great mercy we have been born anew to a living hope through the Resurrection of Jesus Christ from the dead, and to an inheritance which is imperishable.' (1 Pet 1:3-4)

The medieval Jewish commentator Rashi (1040-1105) begins his commentary on Genesis not by commenting on the phrase, 'In the beginning', as we would have expected. Rather, he goes directly to Exodus 12: 'This month shall be for you the beginning of months; it shall be the first month of the year for you.' (Exod 12:2) He comments, referring to the first five books of the Bible, 'the books of the Law of Israel should have commenced with the verse "This month shall be for you the beginning of months" which is the first commandment given to Israel. What is the reason, then, that it commences with the account of the Creation?'

And he goes on to answer by saying that 'this verse calls aloud for explanation in the manner that our rabbis explained it: God created the world for the sake of the Torah which is called "The

---

9. Origen, *Homilies on Genesis*, 1.1. (ACCS 1:1).

beginning of [God's] increase".'[10] (referring to Proverbs 8:22).

This interpretation is dependent, of course, on who is being referred to in this verse of Proverbs. For Rashi it is the Law, for Christians it is certainly Christ. Nevertheless, the point stands. Reno comments:

> The solution rests in specifying the proper sense of 'beginning' ... God is saying, in effect, 'the months and the lunar calendar exist for the sake of marking the time of the Passover'. More bluntly, God is saying to the Israelites as they prepare to depart from Egypt: 'I made time and history for the sake of *this* moment, for the sake of *this* sacrifice'.[11]

We can transfer this insight to the place of this reading within the Easter Vigil: God says to us, 'I made time and history for the sake of *this* moment, for the sake of *this* event: the Resurrection of Christ'. As the *Exsultet* will proclaim of our own coming into being:

> Our birth would have been no gain, had we not been redeemed. ...
> O truly necessary sin of Adam, destroyed completely by the Death of Christ!
> O happy fault that earned so great, so glorious a Redeemer!
> O truly blessed night, worthy alone to know the time and hour when Christ rose from the underworld!

Light without a Need for the Sun

On the first day, God created light and this light creates the morning. We should note how strange this is because there is no sun, moon, or stars until the fourth day. The authors were no fools

---

10. Rashi, in *Chumash with Rashi's Commentary*, ed. A.M. Silbermann (Jerusalem: Silbermann Family, 1934), 2.
11. Reno, 'Beginning,' 35-36.

and, living in a Mediterranean country, they knew that the sun was responsible for light and that in the absence of the sun light diminished or disappeared. This is seen as well in the creation of plant-life on the third day, one day before the creation of the sun. St Basil the Great wrote, 'the adornment of the earth [by plants] is older than the sun, that those who have been misled may cease worshipping the sun as the origin of life'.[12]

Even the mention of evening and morning is somewhat perplexing. Evening and morning are caused by the relative movement of the earth and the sun, so without a sun, how can evening and morning be? In his own recycling of the Genesis story to speak of Christ, St John the Evangelist, in the Prologue to his Gospel, says of the Word that, 'in him was life, and the life was the light of men. The light shines in the darkness.' (John 1:4-5)

The linking of Christ and light from darkness is something which Paul already noted in the letter to the Colossians. God's life is expressed in terms of light, and so also his creation is, first of all, made to reflect the Creator, in being light shining in the dark, formless chaos. In the Nicene Creed, Christ is, as we know, described as 'light from light'. This follows a long biblical tradition. Whereas here God first creates light, God himself is light, as seen when the Psalmist prays, 'lift up the light of your face on us, O Lord!' (Ps 4:7)

This luminosity is contagious from God to Moses, who 'did not know that the skin of his face shone because he had been talking with God'. (Exod 34:29)

But it is in the Gospels that the role of light with reference to God becomes pronounced, especially in the accounts of the Transfiguration, and in the Gospel according to John, where Jesus frequently speaks of himself as light. The light who 'shines in the darkness' and 'was the life of men', as is said of him in Prologue,

12. Basil the Great, *Hexæmeron* 5.1 (ACCS 1:15).

says to those who follow him: 'I am the light of the world; he who follows me will not walk in darkness, but will have the light of life.' (John 8:12)

Christ rises at dawn on the first day. The echo with the first day of creation resounds clearly. Some of the later Fathers of the Church, Bede and Remigius of Auxerre, comment on the unusual timing of the Resurrection given by Matthew: 'After the Sabbath, and towards dawn…'. (Matt 28:1) For them, it is a sign of the light which has dawned in the Resurrection of Christ. 'The usual order of time is not that evening is followed by dawn', says Remigius, 'but darkens into night; these words show that the Lord gave festivity and brilliance to the whole of this night by the light of his Resurrection.'[13]

In God's Image and Likeness

We read that God made humankind in his own image and likeness (1:26-27) by giving them rational minds. Indeed, the creation account in Genesis is precisely the genius of the human mind, pondering the mind that created all things. But on Easter Sunday, when God called the true light of the world to exist anew, and there was a new beginning, the man Jesus Christ was the image of God in a new way, not only in his rational mind, but also in his immortality, a human being no longer subject to death in a new creation. As Melito of Sardis said, and as we live in our readings in the Easter Vigil: 'the mystery of the Passover is new and old, eternal and temporal, corruptible and incorruptible, mortal and immortal…. The law is old, but the Gospel is new; the type was for a time, but grace is forever.'[14]

---

13. Cited by St. Thomas Aquinas, without further reference, *Catena Aurea*, on Matthew 28:1.
14. *Peri Pascha*, 2-4.

First Reading • Genesis 1:1–2:2

Questions for Reflection or Discussion

Re-read the passage with the thought in mind that the story of Creation is also the story of Christ. How does this affect how you experience this text?

What is the significance of the Church choosing this First Reading for the Easter Vigil, at which we celebrate the Lord's resurrection?

2

A Costly Sacrifice

Second Reading • Genesis 22:1-18

LUKE MACNAMARA, O.S.B.

The Context of Creation

The human story of divine encounter from the beginning, through the ages and to the end of time, is taken up in the series of readings at the Easter Vigil. The series opens with the first creation account of Genesis where God speaks, and creation comes into being. From the outset of history, humanity and its world are the product of divine breath and speech. Created in the image and likeness of God, only humanity is empowered with the ability to communicate and thus to enter into a dialogical relationship with God. Creation is ordered towards this goal. The world is specifically designed as a paradise in which humanity may be fruitful and multiply. God's original and enduring intention for humanity is clear, that men and women enjoy full life and bring full life to others. It is good to recall the promise of the beginnings because God will bring his promises to fulfilment. The two prayer options after the First Reading and Psalm each stress both the creation and redemption of humanity. Hearers of this reading at the Vigil are invited to recognise the fulfilment of these promises in the Resurrection of Jesus Christ.

There is a significant gap between the account of creation (Gen 1) and the Second Reading, about Abraham's sacrifice (Gen 22). Humanity sadly rejects the privileged relationship with God in paradise. The intervening chapters of the book of Genesis contain a catalogue of violence and disorder. Divided and dispersed throughout the world, humanity no longer remembers the envisaged peaceful order of the beginnings. The wonderful overture of hopeful promises is now shattered. The proposed sacrifice of Isaac, Abraham's beloved child, threatens to undo the promise. This is a terrible command and projects a horrible image of a vengeful or arbitrary god. However, God does not forget his original purpose and will go to extraordinary lengths to ensure that humanity might possess fullness of life.

A Scandalous Story

Even at the late vigil hour, the account of the near-miss slaying of Isaac by his own father Abraham jolts hearers into paying attention. This is one of the most harrowing stories of the Bible and inspires not only shock, but horror and revulsion. How could God ask of a father that he slay his own son? God might appear harsh and despotic, but the hearers have only recently been present on Good Friday at the celebration of the Lord's Passion. The memory of Jesus' death on the Cross is still fresh. The timing favours reading this story in relation to the Passion with Isaac prefiguring the sacrifice of Christ on the Cross. The story of Isaac, therefore, rather than speaking of a vengeful God, may instead reveal something of the extent of God's love. However, it is important to first hear the story in the context of the book of Genesis.

The account begins with a headline outside the story itself: 'God puts Abraham to the test'. In the story which follows, the characters are unaware of this information. No one knows that this is a test, not Abraham, not Isaac, nor his servants. The headline indicates that the story is not ultimately about Isaac but about Abraham and how he will fare in the test that God puts before him. Abraham has been a central figure in the book of Genesis for ten chapters. He leaves home and kin at the Lord's command (12:1-4) and is blessed with promises of descendants and a land. God changes his name from Abram to Abraham, which signifies 'father of nations' (17:5) and so his very name and identity embody God's promise.

However, Abraham has a chequered career with the Lord, and at several points he suggests alternative ways of ensuring descendants. First, he proposes Eliezer of Damascus. (15:2) His wife Sarah also loses patience and invites her husband to take her slave girl Hagar and so obtain a child by proxy. (16:2) Later, Abraham will propose Ishmael, his child by Hagar, as his heir. (17:18)

There are other questionable elements to Abraham's behaviour. Repeatedly passing off Sarah as his sister to protect himself against Pharaoh (12:10-20) and Abimelech (20:1-18), Abraham seems to doubt God's promises. Nevertheless, the question of the heir seems settled with the birth to Sarah of the long-awaited Isaac. (21:1-3) Now that God has fulfilled this key promise, albeit not yet the promise of the land, what will Abraham's relationship be with God? What has been so longed for is now fulfilled. Is Abraham faithful in his relationship to God only as long as he perceives that he needs him, or does his relationship with God go deeper? Hearers may well have questions about Abraham.

Entering into the Story:
God's Startling Command to Abraham

The story begins with God's calling of Abraham by the name of promise ('father of nations') that God had given him. (17:5) Abraham responds, *'hinneni'* ('here I am'). Abraham demonstrates responsiveness to God, but how far will that responsiveness go when he learns what God is asking of him? God says: 'Take your son, your only child Isaac, whom you love, and go to the land of Moriah. There you shall offer him as a burnt offering on a

Second Reading • Genesis 22:1-18

mountain I will point out to you.' God first highlights Abraham's close bond with Isaac, repeatedly identifying the boy in relation to Abraham: your son, your only child, whom you love. Later, however, God simply designates the boy by the pronoun 'him'. The relation between God and Abraham is at a remove at first where he simply commands him, but towards the end he promises him future communication, indicating where the burnt offering is to take place. There is a shift in the position of Abraham in the short speech of God, moving from being intensely linked with his son to being more closely linked with God.

The command to go forth recalls the beginning of Abraham's relationship with God when he commanded him to go forth from the land of Chaldea. (12:1) Then, Abraham was simply told to go to the land which God would show him. On this occasion, the general location is indicated, the land of Moriah, which can signify either 'place of vision' or 'place of fear' in Hebrew. It is not yet clear as to what sort of place it will turn out to be. However, God will continue to guide Abraham, telling him which mountain to climb for the burnt offering.

What is unclear is who or what is to be offered. The verb of offering may be understood in diverse ways. The command is ambivalent. The Hebrew allows for two interpretations. Is Abraham to offer up his son Isaac, or bring him up so that he can be initiated in the cult? How will Abraham understand the command?

> Lest well-earned love should tempt the faithful sire and seer, to whom his pledge and heir was dear, whom God by chance had given him, to offer him to God (A mighty execution!), there is shown to him a lamb entangled by the head in thorns; a holy victim — holy blood for blood — to God. From whose atoning death, that to the wasted race it might be sign and pledge of safety, signed are with blood their posts and thresholds many — aid immense!
>
> TERTULLIAN, *Of the Harmony of the Old and New Laws*

Should he understand it as initiating Isaac into the cult, it might signify a normalisation of his relationship with God. Should he understand it as offering his son, it would demonstrate his total commitment to God, who has asked everything of him thus far, to leave kith and kin, to go a land which God will show him. Now, however, God is asking something radically different, which goes against the earlier promises of life, and which threatens the very basis of those promises.

The Journey of Three Days

Abraham gets up early in the morning and journeys forth. At an earlier command Abraham left kith and kin for a promise of life and descendants. (12:4) On this occasion the command is accompanied by an intended sacrifice that may possibly negate the earlier promise. How will Abraham understand the divine command? Is God requesting an act of thanksgiving for Isaac on the mountain, or is God asking for a much greater relationship, an offering of some part of himself, something intimately united to himself?

While Abraham appears to obey readily, the storyteller is laconic. Abraham shows no emotion. The account is at first very mundane. Donkeys are always saddled for journeys. The surprise is that it is Abraham who saddles his donkey and not the two boys whom he later takes with him, and that he himself splits the wood for the burnt offering. Abraham was commanded to take his son, but he takes two servant boys along with him and, afterwards, Isaac. (22:3) His son is mentioned last, as something of an afterthought. Is Abraham distancing himself from his son in preparation to offer him up, or does the late choice of Isaac indicate Abraham's reluctance to bring him to be slaughtered?

The story speeds up. On the third day of the journey Abraham looks up and sees the place in the distance. (22:4) Much has happened in silence. The tension rises as the place of the sacrifice is

Second Reading • Genesis 22:1-18

now in view. Abraham tells the two boys to stay behind with the donkeys while the boy (referring to his son) and he will go ahead. Abraham uses the same term to describe his son as that used by the storyteller for his two servants – 'boy', without any possessive pronoun. The son appears more distant to his father than the boys in his service. Abraham reports to the youths what he and Isaac will do. They will go over there and worship and then return. (22:5) An act of worship is to take place, but it is not clear what this will involve. A note of hope emerges for the fate of Isaac in that Abraham says that they will both return.

Abraham takes the wood for the burnt offering and places it on Isaac, who is unlikely to make good ground with such a burden. Moreover, by carrying the wood, he truly becomes what Abraham has just said of him, one of his servant boys and no longer his son. The close association with the wood hints at his sacrifice where, instead of being under the wood, he will be placed upon it. Abraham carries the fire and knife, and this suggests that it is he who will slay the victim and set the wood alight. The elements which point to the future sacrifice also point to the possible roles of Isaac as victim and of Abraham as the one who offers up the victim. The pair travel together.

On the way, Isaac speaks for the first time. He calls Abraham 'my father', recalling the affectionate language of God's initial command, 'your son your only child, whom you love'. Abraham acknowledges their relationship as he calls Isaac 'my son'. The strong intimate bond is emphasised as they walk together. Abraham's first word *'hinneni'* ('here I am')[1] recalls his earlier response to God. There is a consistency to his readiness to respond, both to God and to his son. Isaac raises the obvious question – but how forceful it is from his mouth: 'Behold the fire and the wood but where is the lamb for the burnt offering?' (22:7)

---
1. This is translated simply as 'yes' in the lectionary text.

Isaac, the potential victim, raises the question of what is to be sacrificed. For Isaac it is simply that a lamb is lacking, but for the hearers of this story the tragic dilemma for Abraham is in view. His response to Isaac, that God will provide a lamb for the burnt offering, can be interpreted diversely. While for Isaac it is evasive, for hearers, it may indicate a supreme confidence on Abraham's part that God will provide a lamb, or an acceptance that the lamb is his own son. The dialogue concludes with the refrain: the two of them went on together. The physical proximity belies the cognitive distance between them. The father cannot speak of the decision which he is grappling with. Isaac is left to wonder at what Abraham will do.

The Sacrifice

When they arrive, Isaac fades from view as the storyteller concentrates on Abraham and his actions. There is a progressive slowing of time, the building of an altar, the laying out of the wood, the binding of Isaac, the placing of him on the altar, the extending of the hand, the taking of the knife. There is no delay, simply a logical and progressive carrying out of the necessary tasks for a sacrifice. The journey took more than three days and is recounted after the fact, but here, each recounted action takes progressively less time and so the intensity of the focus increases. Building the altar takes some hours perhaps, the laying out of the wood perhaps half an hour, the binding of Isaac some ten minutes, placing him on the altar above the wood some two minutes.

The final actions are recounted as they take place, the stretching out of the hand and the taking of the knife. Attention rests on the knife poised to slaughter Isaac, as evidenced in the artistic representations of this scene by the Renaissance masters, Caravaggio (1603), Domenichino (1627) and Rembrandt (1635).

The prolonged account may indicate that Abraham is stalling

in the hope that God may intervene, or it may indicate how determined he is to fulfil the divine command. The building of an altar at Moriah recalls his first building of an altar at Moreh, when he arrived in Canaan following an appearance of the Lord to him. (12:6-7) This first altar was a response of faith to the promise of descendants and land. (12:1-3) Now, this second altar points to his trust in God, and indicates his agreement to God's request of him.

The binding of Isaac emphasises Abraham's determination, and flight for Isaac is now impossible. The extending of the hand to slaughter Isaac leaves no doubt as to Abraham's determination to fulfil the stricter interpretation of the divine command. However, the prolonged account, the meticulous and careful action, the delay by performing all the preparatory tasks by himself perhaps presage a confidence that God will intervene.

The Intervention of the Angel of the Lord and the Sacrifice of the Ram

The question at this point is no longer whether Abraham will obey this incomprehensible divine command, but whether the child of the promise will survive. The tension is at a crescendo when the angel of the Lord intervenes. The intervention of the angel doesn't diminish the tension but joins it at its peak moment. It is not yet clear how Abraham will respond.

The angel calls out to Abraham. He does not seize his arm which would have been a sure way to save Isaac. Instead, he calls out to him twice using the name that God gave him: 'Abraham, Abraham', which evokes God's initial command to perform the sacrifice. Although busy in fulfilling God's command as he understands it, he responds to God as he did at first: *'hinneni'* ('here I am'). He demonstrates, despite the dramatic trial that he is undergoing, his adherence to God, his continuing openness to God's word and his readiness to respond to it.

The angel replies: 'Do not raise your hand against the boy. Do not harm him, for now I know you fear God. You have not refused me your son, your only son.' (22:12) There is a shift in how the angel refers to Isaac, which reflects a shift in Abraham's relationship with Isaac. When God spoke to Abraham of Isaac, he identified him as 'your son, your only child, whom you love, Isaac', but now the angel simply refers to Isaac as 'the boy'.

By raising the knife Abraham shows that he no longer holds the boy for himself but is willing to return to God what is God's own gift. Abraham, in response to God's inexplicable command, relinquishes the strong bond with Isaac, recalled by references at the end as 'your son, your only son'. Abraham's relationship with God is not based on calculation, on taking for his own God's gifts and building an inheritance independently of God. This is expressed by the angel in traditional terms: 'Now I know you fear God.' Abraham looks up and sees a ram caught in a bush. (22:13) There is a close correlation between the verbs 'to fear' and 'to see' in Hebrew. Abraham who fears God, now also sees. He takes the ram and does precisely with it as God has told him to do with his son Isaac. (22:2) Abraham now enacts the ritual sacrifice in place of his son, according to the divine command.

The Re-naming of the Place

The general location was initially called the land of Moriah (22:2), a place of fear or a place of vision. Fear has been central to this story, both the very real fear about the possible death of Isaac but also fear of God. However, the verb 'to fear' in reference to God carries connotations of reverence, respect and love rather than terror. Isaac, the long-promised child of God, was born when Abraham was already 100 years old and his wife Sarah was advanced in age. (21:5-6) Isaac would never have been born without God's intervention. Abraham's *fear* of God has grown since he left the

Second Reading • Genesis 22:1-18

land of the Chaldeans, and despite the seemingly irrational command to sacrifice Isaac, he trusts that God keeps his promises of life, descendants and a homeland. Moriah is well named as a place of fear, but of a fear transformed from one of dread to one of love that knows no cost.

Seeing has also had an important role at various stages of the story. The storyteller speaks of Abraham seeing: he sees the mountain from afar (22:4) and sees the ram. (22:13) When Abraham speaks he does not focus on his own seeing but on God's: 'God will see.' (22:8, 14)[2]

> And so too God revealed a mystery, great and marvellous, to his friend Abraham. For through the sacrifice he became a priest; while by the type he made him a prophet. And God Most High made known to him that he too would give his only Son for the world's sake, so that God become man might save the human race from error.
>
> ST EPHREM
> *Sermon on Abraham and Isaac*

In the first instance, Isaac asks where is the animal to be sacrificed and to this Abraham replies that God will see (to it). There is an implied object, a projected animal for sacrifice, even if at this point none is present, unless possibly Isaac himself. Abraham cannot himself see how things will go, but he places his trust in God's seeing.

The answer to Isaac's poignant question, 'God will see', remains a mystery for Isaac and for Abraham at this point. It is this very inability to see the outcome that proves Abraham's trust. At the conclusion of the ordeal, Abraham renames the place 'the Lord will see'. The tense and the absence of an obvious object indicate a renewed trust in God's promise for the future. God will continue to be providentially involved in the life of Abraham, Isaac and their descendants.

2. The lectionary text has 'God will provide'. The Hebrew verb 'to see' is typically translated as 'to provide' in order to facilitate the translation but the text should be struggled with as it stands.

There is an aside from the storyteller explaining the ongoing tradition about the name of the place: 'Hence the saying today: on the mountain the Lord will be seen.'[3] Abraham climbed a mountain where he expects that God will see, and when there he discovers that God is seen. By responding to God's inexplicable command and placing his trust in him, Abraham comes to a place where God is seen. The storyteller's aside opens the story to the hearers. There is no specification about the mountain where God will be seen and so it could be any mountain for those who, like Abraham, offer God life. Hearers are invited to be seen by God and to see God by imitating Abraham's behaviour and response of faith.

Second Conclusion

It is unusual for a messenger of God to speak a second time. It seems as if the scene has concluded and yet something more needs to be said. Abraham recognises that in the angel, it is God who has made himself visible. The angel speaks again, but with God's own words. The language is hyperbolic. The promise goes beyond Isaac and includes Abraham's entire progeny. The promise extends to the entire universe – heaven, sea, earth – recalling God's earlier promises. (13:16; 15:5) Abraham's offspring will possess the land by inheritance rather than conquest and they will be a blessing for those they rule over.

The attitude of Abraham towards his son, not one of selfish possession, allows for a fruitful reign for all. The earlier promises of descendants (Gen 12:1-3) were dependant on leaving country and kin, but now there is a solemn oath, with no condition. Abraham's attentive listening and ready response to God's voice ('*hinneni*' – 'here I am') has permitted this – a listening which

---

3. Again, the lectionary translates the Hebrew verb 'to see' by 'provide'. The lectionary text has 'God will provide'.

began and concluded the episode and was crucial to the outcome. This composite Hebrew word, *hinneni*, resonated strongly with the poet, songwriter and artist, Leonard Cohen (1934-2016) and forms part of a refrain in the lead track of his final album *You Want It Darker* (2016). The refrain goes: '*Hinneni, hinneni*, I'm ready, my Lord.' Although this word occurs on several occasions in the Hebrew Bible, Cohen surely points to Abraham's repeated use of *hinneni* when he says: 'That declaration of readiness, no matter what the outcome, that's a part of everyone's soul ... It's only when the emergency becomes articulate that we can locate that willingness to serve.'[4] Abraham, in the midst of his trials, managed to hear God speak both at the beginning and, importantly, through the angel at the crucial moment. The divine-human communication which originated in creation is restored and leads to life even in the face of death.

The Responsorial Psalm and Prayer

The refrain of the Psalm which follows the reading at the Easter Vigil, 'Preserve me. God, I take refuge in you', might have been spoken by both Isaac and Abraham. Both have escaped from disaster – for Isaac, death; and for Abraham, the destruction of the promise of descendants. Hearers might identify closely with Abraham's relief at this point and pray this psalm with him, but it may also evoke near-miss episodes in their own lives where they give thanks for God's intervention at the ninth hour. While Isaac has avoided death, the psalmist speaks of actual death: 'For you will not leave my soul among the dead, nor let your beloved know decay.' This psalm is prayed by one who experiences death but who also trusts in God's power to bring back to life: 'You will

---

4. From the October 13, 2016 You Want It Darker Press Event (L.A.) https://cohencentric.com/2016/10/28/hineni-declaration-readiness-no-matter-outcome-thats-part-everyones-soul-leonard-cohen/

show me the path of life, the fullness of joy in your presence.' As the refrain is repeated, it gathers force. 'Preserve me, God, I take refuge in you', no longer applies simply to avoiding death but to breaking free from death and returning to life.

The psalm extends beyond this story of Abraham and Isaac, for neither died. Instead, it takes up their story but links it with Jesus in whom it is fulfilled. The celebration of Jesus' Passion on Good Friday recalls that whereas Isaac is spared, Jesus dies on the Cross. Jesus undergoes death to break the power of death. From the stillness of the underworld on Holy Saturday, Jesus may be imagined praying this psalm for himself and for all those who will follow him into death. At his rising, Jesus may again pray this psalm, attesting to the fulfilment of God's promise for himself but also for all who will follow him.

The accompanying prayer provides a concluding synthesis, specifically mentioning Abraham who 'through the Paschal Mystery' becomes father of nations. The mystery may obviously refer to the death and Resurrection of Jesus, in which Abraham participates by accepting to sacrifice Isaac. However, God accomplishes the sacrifice of the Beloved Son and raises him to new life. Despite the imminent threat to Isaac, Abraham's faith in God's powerful promise results in a multitude of descendants.

The term 'Paschal Mystery' or 'Sacrament' in the Latin text may also refer to the principal paschal sacrament celebrated at the Easter Vigil, namely Baptism.[5] The Vigil is the privileged time of year for Baptism.[6] Those about to be baptised through the rite of Baptism enter among the faithful and also take their place in a new enlarged family. Throughout the world new members are

---

5. The Latin text has *'per paschale sacramentum'*. This term refers both to the Paschal Mystery, the death and resurrection of Jesus but also the Paschal Sacrament par excellence, namely Baptism. See Patrick Regan, 'Paschal Vigil: Passion and Passage' *Worship* 79 (2005): 116.
6. See *Rite of Christian Initiation of Adults* no.23.

Second Reading • Genesis 22:1-18

added to the family of the faithful, through the grace of adoption.

Many read the sacrifice of Isaac and that of the ram typologically, as prefiguring Christ's sacrifice on the Cross. However, the Vigil points elsewhere. The emphasis in the story of Abraham and Isaac rests firmly upon the father. While Isaac may die, the stress is upon the father's journey of faith. Although a lamb is initially envisaged for the sacrifice by both father and son, ultimately it is a ram – the father of a lamb – that is sacrificed. The lectionary's title 'The sacrifice of Abraham, our father in faith' rightly stresses that it is Abraham's sacrifice.

If this be the case, then the traditional Christological typology of this passage ought to be expanded to include a theological typology: Abraham may prefigure God who accepts to offer up his Son. Whereas the request to sacrifice Isaac, even if only a test for Abraham, presented a scandalous vision of a despotic God, if we understand the story more as being about the sacrifice of Abraham, God can be seen as seeking to demonstrate the extent of his own love for humanity and the fruit of that love. When the sacrifice of his Son Jesus is accomplished on the Cross and Jesus rises on the third day, the depths of that love and its fruit become visible.

Questions for Reflection or Discussion

Who suffers more in this story, Abraham or Isaac?

What does this reading reveal about the nature of God's love for his people?

3

Crossing the Red Sea

Third Reading • Exodus 14:15–15:1

FRANCIS COUSINS

Introduction

The Third Reading from the Easter Vigil tells the story of how God led his people from slavery to freedom through the waters of the Red Sea. The reading is central to the book of Exodus, being the key event in that story, and also provides a hinge for the dynamic of the liturgy of the Easter Triduum. The events of the reading follow the celebration of the first Passover meal (Holy Thursday); the account of the ten plagues culminating in the death of the firstborn of all Egypt, which carries echoes not only of the binding of Isaac (Gen 22), but also of the liturgy of Good Friday; and the crossing of the sea calls to mind the Baptisms which are celebrated as part of the Easter Vigil. The Exodus from Egypt, which brings the Hebrews from slavery to a new life of freedom, echoes the themes of the Easter Vigil, where people pass from death or sin to new life, embodied by passing through the waters of Baptism.

The crossing of the sea acts as the climax of the first part of Exodus, as the people of Israel leave behind their lives of slavery in the land of Egypt and begin the journey to the Promised Land. This chapter shall focus on some key elements: the identity of the Lord as a warrior, salvation by the sea, hardening Pharaoh's heart, the role of the angel of the Lord, Moses stretching out his hand, the Lord saving Israel, and the transition to the Song of the Sea.

Third Reading • Exodus 14:15–15:1

The Narrative Setting and Some Historical Background

The Book of Exodus begins with the Hebrews living under conditions of slavery in Egypt. Moses, whose miraculous birth is narrated in Exodus 2, is called by God to lead the people of Israel and to demand that Pharaoh let his people go – a phrase which echoes throughout the book.[1] Pharaoh refuses this request, which leads to a series of plagues, culminating in a final plague, the death of the firstborn, which ultimately presents the Hebrews with an opportunity to flee the Egyptians. The plagues narrate a battle between the Lord of Israel and the Pharaoh, whose original question to Moses, 'Who is the Lord that I should heed him and let Israel go?' (Exod 5:2) is answered indirectly in demonstrations of power. The Lord controls nature, as shown in the plagues, and proves that his power is greater than the might of Egypt.

The text shows the importance of viewing the Lord as one who is on the side of the weak and oppressed. Egypt was the superpower of the day, and, confronted with a group of migrants who were overworked as slaves, Egypt fell to a mighty defeat, despite having the military might of chariots, horsemen, and the whole of Pharaoh's army on their side. Exodus tells of the extraordinary actions of God which liberate the Israelites. It is through God's actions, which stir the faith of the Israelites (see 14:31), that we learn about who God is.

The narrative of Exodus 14 describes events in concrete, specific terms. We are told the Israelites crossed the sea, walking between walls of water; and we are left with the impression of a tidal wave, which returned and engulfed the Egyptians. There are a few distinctive elements in Exodus 14, such as the role of the pillars of cloud and fire, and the east wind. Moses stretches out his hands

---

1. The phrase occurs nine times (5:1; 7:14; 8:1, 20, 21; 9:1, 13; 10:3, 4).

firstly so that the waters are divided and the Israelites can pass dryshod through the waters, and then a second time causing the waters to return, which then close upon the Egyptians who follow.

Sometimes, by getting caught up in historical questions, the dynamic of the narrative is lost. Historians ask questions such as 'Who was the Pharaoh?' 'Where exactly did the people go?' 'What sea did they cross?' 'Was it just marshy land?' 'Was there a miracle at all?' One can try and explain away the miraculous side of the narrative. Maybe the action of the sea corresponds to the rising and falling tides, or shallow waters being blown back by the wind, or both. Hypothetically, an army in pursuit could naturally be caught by the tide. The narrative tells us, after all, that the Egyptian chariots were stuck in the mud and engulfed by the returning waters. However, the narrative also explicitly states that miraculously the waters were split and stood up like walls. (14:16, 22, 29)

> The message of Passover remains as powerful as ever. Freedom is won not on the battlefield but in the classroom and the home. Teach your children the history of freedom if you want them never to lose it.
>
> CHIEF RABBI JONATHAN SACKS

The first concern of the text is not historicity as we understand it. The story is a theophany. It reveals the Lord to the Israelites, to the defeated Egyptians, and indeed to the reader. In the story of the plot to kill the firstborn sons of the Israelites, it is not the Pharaoh who is named, but rather the two midwives of the Hebrews, Shiphrah and Puah. (1:15) This is of no help to historians (much to their chagrin) but points to how the narrative wishes to honour the weak and not the strong. It is not interested in placing the narrative in the context of the world stage, as Luke does, for example, in the introduction to his Gospel. Rather it narrates the beginnings of a people, and the role of the Lord in this story.

Third Reading • Exodus 14:15–15:1

In Exodus, the power of the Lord is revealed again and again through natural events. Each of the plagues could have a 'natural' explanation, and the magicians of Pharaoh do manage to recreate them, allowing Pharaoh not to relent and recognise the power of the Lord. But simply having a natural explanation is not enough. Exodus wishes to tell us who the Lord is (see 5:2) and to demonstrate the power of the Lord, and his care and concern for the Israelites. The plagues show that the Lord can control nature, but also in the tenth and most deadly plague, the death of the firstborn, that the Lord has control over life and death.

In the face of this, Pharaoh relents and allows the Israelites to go free, only to change his mind and pursue them. This foolhardy and impulsive action leads to the final demonstration of the Lord's power to the Egyptians, as he controls the waters through which the Israelites pass safely to a life of freedom, and which crash down on the Egyptians causing their death.

The final plague also echoes the decree of Pharaoh at the beginning of the book of Exodus, where, worried that the Hebrews are becoming too great in number, he decrees that all Hebrew male infants should be killed at birth. Whereas this plot failed, a failure which led to the birth of Moses, the Lord's power is manifest in the passing of the angel of death over Egypt, which ultimately leads to the deliverance of the Israelites. It is this deliverance which is celebrated at Passover, the meal which Jesus and his disciples ate on Holy Thursday.

Who Is the Lord? A Mighty Warrior?

The text presents the Lord as a warrior. The idea that gods are warriors was important in the Ancient Near East. The Lord helps Israel defeat their enemies. Yet, this is unlike other 'holy wars'. In this battle, it is the Lord who fights on behalf of Israel, almost unbidden. The Israelites tremble, being passive, almost unknowing, participants as the Lord fights for them in an unequal contest with the Egyptians. Indeed, it is actually the Egyptians who are the first to acknowledge that the Lord is fighting for the Israelites. (14:25) Only at the end, having seen the great work that the Lord has done, do the Israelites fear the Lord and believe in him. (14:31)

For the contemporary reader this image of the Lord as a warrior can disturb their image of God. In the context of Exodus, it is the power of God as a warrior that gives hope to people in slavery, and has continued to give hope to people suffering oppression down through the centuries. Warrior-gods were also thought to act on behalf of the powerful, which can support an oppressive view of the world. In Exodus, the warrior God is on the side of the weak and those living in bondage, a fact that continues to inspire liberation movements. Civil rights movements in the USA and in Northern Ireland drew inspiration from this idea of God being on the side of the oppressed, leading people from slavery to freedom. And while today we might naturally be drawn to see ourselves on the side of the Lord and the people of Israel, it is good to reflect on where we truly find ourselves in the story. We might baulk at the idea that we could be the Egyptians, but sometimes reality bites!

Salvation of the Sea

The sea is the location for a final confrontation between the Lord and (the army of) Pharaoh. The transition to this stage is found in 14:5-7, 9a, where Pharaoh decides to pursue the Israelites whom he has cast out from the land. The narrative focuses less on the crossing of the sea than on the Lord's control of the sea, which ultimately destroys the Egyptians. On two occasions the sea becomes the object of direct action, as the Lord first sends an east wind on it and then dries it; (14:21) and once the subject, when it returns to its natural flow, in the process destroying the

Third Reading • Exodus 14:15–15:1

Egyptian army. (14:27) The power of the water, at the service of the Lord, both gives life and takes life. The Lord is the one 'who alone stretched out the heavens and trampled the waves of the sea'. (Job 9:8)

The power over the sea links back to two foundational narratives from the early chapters of Genesis: in the creation account (Gen 1), the Lord demonstrates power over the waters in creating the earth; and in the Flood Narrative (Gen 7), the Lord destroys the earth with a flood. The creative and destructive powers of the waters are harnessed by the Lord, who brings about the destruction of the Egyptians and the salvation of the Israelites.

There are echoes of the First Reading of the Vigil (Gen 1:1-2:2) in the Lord splitting the waters, with the act of separation reminiscent of the act of creation. These waters will later teem with life, irrigate the earth and make it yield abundant fruit. Within the context of the Easter Vigil, the passage of the people of Israel through water to salvation recalls the salvific features of water, during a liturgy when new members are often welcomed into the community by Baptism, and all present are invited to renew their baptismal promises.

> You too, if you distance yourself from the Egyptians and flee far from the power of demons, will see what great helps will be provided to you each day and what great protection is available to you. All that is asked of you is that you stand firm in the faith and do not let yourself be terrified by either the Egyptian cavalry or the noise of their chariots.
>
> ORIGEN, *Homily on Exodus*

There is also, as in Genesis 1, a strong interplay between light and darkness, which is controlled by the Lord. The natural darkness and cold is alleviated by the pillar of fire, the excessive brightness and heat of the day by the pillar of cloud. The Lord continuously shelters his people. In the dark night of the Vigil all the baptised light candles, which represent the light of Christ, foreshadowed in Exodus by the burning bush and the pillar of fire.

Our reading picks up the story as the Egyptian army are advancing on the Israelites, with Moses in position as the mediator between God and the people. They are in a state of distress and cry out. The people and their leaders first cried to Pharaoh in their distress for relief from their oppression (5:8, 15), while Moses addressed his cries to the Lord. (8:8) Now, the people finally address their cry for help to the Lord. (14:10) Even if the Lord's response 'Why do you cry to me?' seems a little abrupt, he directs the people, and Moses, to the proper course of action. (14:15)

Why are the people crying out? Previously, the Israelites were complaining to Moses as they became greatly frightened, asking: 'Was it for want of graves in Egypt that you brought us out to die in the wilderness?' (14:11) The mention of the wilderness highlights the desolation felt by the people and the realisation that they are really in the middle of nowhere.

The people's fear of death highlights the fact that they don't perceive God's purpose in this journey, which is to bring them to freedom and life. Such incomprehension and complaining will mark the journey to the Promised Land. This is sometimes called the murmuring motif.[2] They even begin to invent tales of 'I told you so', suggesting that they had warned Moses this would happen before they left. The complaints of the people once again place Moses in the position of mediator between the people and the Lord. They address their complaints to Moses, who in turn reassures them that 'the Lord will fight for you'. (14:14)

Hardening Pharaoh's Heart

In our text, verse 17 tells us that the Lord will make the Egyptians

---

2. See Exod 15:24; 16:2-3; 17:2-3; Num 11:4-6; 14:2-3; 16:13-14; 20:2-5; 21:4-5; Deut 1:27-28.

stubborn, though a more literal translation of the original Hebrew text reads: 'I for my part will make the heart of the Egyptians so stubborn that they will follow them.' Here, the Hebrew syntax suggests an immediacy and intensity in the hardening. The Greek translation adds 'the heart of Pharaoh and all the Egyptians', marking the symbolic position of Pharaoh as the head of the Egyptians, and stressing the parallel relationship between the Lord and the people of Israel.

The narrative of Exodus 14 has already mentioned the hardening of Pharaoh's heart in verses 8-9, even though Pharaoh has already decided to give chase (verses 5-7). Again in verse 17, the Lord states that he will harden the hearts of the Egyptians. The hardening of Pharaoh's heart reflects a theme which is woven like a thread through the early chapters of Exodus. (See 4:21; 7:3) It occurs 20 times, some stating 'his heart was hardened', (7:13, 22) a use of the divine passive which serves to underlines the Lord's absolute control over events.

The concept of the Lord being in control of events is apparent, but such control can raise questions for the contemporary reader: Could God have softened Pharaoh's heart? Does it take away Pharaoh's free will? The answers to such questions are not easy. Nor should they be. Here, I can offer a few starting points for reflection.

Reading the narrative as a whole, focusing on its literary elements, and how it connects with the wider story of the Israelites being led from slavery in Egypt, one notes that the hardening motif is closely connected to the ten plagues which preceded Pharaoh's decision to let the people go. Despite the hardships suffered by Pharaoh, and the people of Egypt as a whole, the signs did not achieve their goal. There was still more drama to come, with the images of the Egyptian chariots following the fleeing Israelites adding to that drama. It seems that Pharaoh will never learn, 'Who is the Lord?'[3] His stubborn nature leads him to go back on his word and pursue the Israelites into the sea, despite all he has seen and heard. Put this way, the hardening of Pharaoh's heart is not a theological dilemma, but a literary motif.[4]

Ultimately, Pharaoh is responsible for his hard heart, even if God hardened it. The character of Pharaoh is at best aloof, at worst indifferent to the suffering of not only the Israelites, but also his own people who bear the brunt of the plagues. Indeed, it is only when the plagues strike directly at the house of Pharaoh that he finally relents and allows the Israelites to go.

That the Lord is in control of events does not lessen human responsibility. It is a most human response to seek to set the blame for actions at the door of another. Humankind's responsibility for actions and their consequences is a prominent biblical theme. From the story of Adam and Eve in the garden, where they learn the consequences of disobeying the Lord, a theme develops across the Pentateuch where good things happen to good people, while bad things happen to bad people. While, ultimately, this theological outlook is found wanting (Job being one memorable example of a good person railing against the injustice of his life), this outlook does cultivate a strong sense of human responsibility. While Pharaoh might ultimately want to blame the Lord for his problems, an all too human reaction, he could also reflect on the missed opportunities to do the right thing and let the people go.

The Angel of the Lord

The angel of the Lord, and the pillar of cloud, which have been leading the Israelites, move to the back of the column, to separate the people of Israel and their Egyptian pursuers. The angel of the

---

3. See Exodus 5:2, a key question for all readers of Exodus.
4. Brevard Childs, *The Book of Exodus*, OTL (Louisville: Westminster, 1974), 173–74.

Lord was identified with the divine presence and first appeared to Moses in the flame of the burning bush (3:2). Later, the divine presence is manifested in a pillar of cloud by day and pillar of fire by night which constantly accompanies the people in their desert journey (13:21-22). The pillar, therefore, may be viewed as a physical manifestation of the divine presence with the Israelites.

At the angel of the Lord's reappearance, he is again closely associated with the divine presence, manifested in the pillar of cloud (14:19). It is not only the angel, but the Lord himself, who is present with his people. The angel's primary function is to lead the people of Israel in the wilderness. However, at this juncture, the angel and the pillar of cloud move to the rear of the group of Israelites to act as a protective barrier, separating the camp of the Israelites from the camp of the Egyptians. Since the cloud provides both light and darkness, some Jewish commentary has suggested that it made the Egyptian side dark, while the Israelite side remained light. Its main function, however, it to keep the two sides apart, and thus keep the Israelites safe.

The presence of the Lord in the pillar of cloud will later be manifest in the tent of meeting and the ark of the covenant, which the people carry with them in their journey through the wilderness, and which is placed in the sanctuary at the dedication of the Temple in Jerusalem. Throughout the journey to the Promised Land there remains a strong sense that the Lord is with Israel, literally and metaphorically.

Moses Stretches out His Hand

Through the outstretched hand of Moses the power of the Lord is shown to act and assert control over nature. In 14:8, we read that the Israelites went out 'with raised arm', suggestive of an act undertaken with power. Moses was told to 'raise your staff and stretch out your hand over the sea and part it'. (14:16) When he did, 'the Lord drove back the sea with a strong easterly wind all night'. (14:21) And when he stretched out his hand after the Israelites had safely passed, the sea returned to its normal state. (14:26-27)

These three moments demonstrate the power that comes from Moses raising his arms. While Moses' actions are physical indications, it is the power of the Lord which is at work. In a later episode in Exodus, Moses' outstretched arms play a key role in a battle against Amalek (17:9-13). While the Israelites engaged their enemies, as long as Moses' hands were raised the Israelites prevailed. When he grows weary the Amalekites begin to prevail, so Aaron and Hur assist him by holding his hands aloft so that Israel may prevail. The raising of the hands allows the exercise of the power of the Lord.

In our reading, at the second stretching out of Moses's hand, all the chariots and charioteers, the whole army of Pharaoh indeed, were covered by the returning sea. The chariots are a symbol for the Egyptian army; moreover, they are a sign of the power of the army, numbering 600 chosen chariots, and all the chariots of Egypt. The repetition underscores the strength of the force which the Lord has overcome. There would seem to be no comparison, at least on human terms, between the two forces: chariots versus outstretched hand. Yet, it is the latter which emerges victorious. The Hebrew word for hand (*yad*) also translates as 'power,' a double meaning which the author of the text uses to great effect.

Finally in 14:31, the Hebrew literally reads, 'and the Israelites saw the great arm, which the Lord did in Egypt'. This verse suggests that power comes from the hand of God, an important motif in biblical literature. In Deuteronomy's retelling of the Exodus story, it is God's outstretched arm (and not that of Moses) which is the source of power and which leads the people out of Egypt. (Deut 4:34; 5:15) The Deuteronomy narrative makes explicit that it was the hand of the Lord which caused Israel to prevail.

Many Church Fathers have seen the raised arms of Moses as prefiguring Christ's outstretched arms on the Cross. The salvation won by the outstretching of the prophet's arms for Israel foreshadows the salvation brought to the whole world through Christ.

The Lord Saves Israel

The confrontation at the sea does not really require Israel's participation; they are in fact commanded to be passive: 'be still'. (14:14) The action occurs in two stages: first, the Lord instructs Moses to stretch out his hand so as to control the sea, which allows Israel to escape, while setting up the attack against the Egyptian army; second, Moses is to stretch out his hand again so as to release the sea and destroy the pursuing Egyptians.

The destruction of the Egyptian army is more than a plague. It is a salvation event. In 14:13, the Israelites are told that they will see the salvation of the Lord. This is repeated at the conclusion of the event: 'The Lord saved Israel that day.' (14:30) It also becomes a central motif in the Song of the Sea. 'The Lord is salvation.' (15:2) The emphasis on salvation and the destruction of the Egyptian army is viewed in this light. The purpose of the account is to demonstrate God's willingness and ability to save his people against such insurmountable odds.

God is master of his creation, and shows care for that creation. God uses the natural means of nature to carry out the miraculous splitting of the sea. The plan has been outlined in 14:4: 'I will harden Pharaoh's heart, and he will pursue them, so that I will gain glory for myself over Pharaoh and all his army; and the Egyptians shall know that I am the Lord.' Such a plan also links back to Pharaoh's question in 5:2: 'Who is the Lord, that I should heed him and let Israel go? I do not know the Lord, and I will not let Israel go.'

The narrative of the first 15 chapters of Exodus responds to this question. The Lord, the God of Israel, is one who cares for the people of Israel, who were slaves in a foreign land. The Creator God (Lord) has power over nature, as demonstrated in the ten plagues, over life and death (the tenth plague), even over the chaotic waters of the Red Sea and not only over the people of Israel, but also over Egypt, as seen in the Lord's ability to harden Pharaoh's heart.

One of the other ways in which the Lord demonstrates power is in control over the Egyptians. In addition to hardening their hearts, the Lord states, 'I will gain glory through Pharaoh, his army and his horsemen'. In addition to power over nature, the Lord also demonstrates power over the Egyptians, the enemies of Israel. It is the Lord who locks the wheels of the chariots of the Egyptians, (14:25) which causes the Egyptians to panic in realisation that the Lord is truly fighting on the side of the Israelites.

It is striking that it is the Egyptians who first acknowledge the role of the Lord in the battle. It is only in the final verse of chapter 14, when the battle is over and the Israelites see the dead of the Egyptians on the shore, that the Israelites come to fear the Lord and have faith in him and his servant Moses, because they have seen the Lord's wondrous power. Despite all the wonders the Lord has worked, it is the Egyptians who first come to recognise his power.

The closing verses provide an interpretation of the Exodus event. The promised salvation of the Lord has been achieved. The people believe in the Lord, and the prediction from the commission of Moses, that the people would believe that the God of Abraham, Isaac and Jacob has appeared to Moses (4:1, 5, 8-9, 31) came to pass. The Lord has also heard the cry of the people of Israel and delivered them from bondage in Egypt.

Third Reading • Exodus 14:15–15:1

The Transition to the Song of the Sea

The opening line of chapter 15 provides a transition to the Song of the Sea. The hymn extols the virtues of the Lord as warrior, and the people of Israel exult that the Lord has defeated their enemies. In the context of the Easter Vigil, through the waters of Baptism, God forms a new family of Christian people, set free from the slavery of sin. The Song of Exodus 15 could also be read, in continuity with Exodus 14, as a celebration of this triumph. The Song of the Sea is a celebration of the Lord's salvific power; it tells the story of a victory over both earthly forces (15:6) and cosmic forces (15:11), which makes it particularly appropriate for the liturgical setting of the Easter Vigil.

Conclusion

The Third Reading from the Easter Vigil tells one of the most important stories in the history of the people of Israel, and carries many echoes of the Christian story. The crossing of the Red Sea sets the contours for what God means by redemption. God is willing and able to deliver God's people, and this provides the basis for hope in the face of current and future threats. Contemporary society can cut God off from natural phenomena. While this raises questions about us, about God, and about our relationship with God, it is important to pay attention to the details of the story of the crossing of the sea. While the idea of a warrior God may provoke consternation for today's reader, who might more easily relate to the Lord's presence on the side of the oppressed, to remove uncomfortable elements from the text does an injustice to the story.

The power of the story lies in Moses leading the people of Israel to freedom against all odds, showing the power of the Lord against the mighty armies of Pharaoh, which leads the people of Israel to believe in the Lord and his servant Moses. The mighty superpower Egypt has been toppled and the migrant people, working as slaves in a foreign land, have been saved. The magnitude of what the Lord does for Israel cannot be overstated. In the Easter Vigil, we continue to remember this salvific event, and its place in the history of salvation, as we gather to celebrate the Resurrection of Jesus, whom God raised from the dead.

Questions for Reflection or Discussion

How does the idea of God as a warrior, fighting on the side of the oppressed, speak to our contemporary world and its societies?

What parallels can you see between the passage of the Israelites from slavery to freedom and the passage of Jesus from death to life?

4

Discovering God in the Desert
Fourth Reading • Isaiah 54:5-14

JESSIE ROGERS

Introduction

The poet-prophet of Isaiah 54 paints pictures of hope across a very bleak landscape. The words evoke a turning-point with their promise of restoration, return and redemption. Notice the sadness in the phrases that describe the present situation: 'a forsaken wife, distressed in spirit', (Isa 54:6) and 'unhappy creature, storm-tossed, disconsolate'. (54:11) There are allusions to a terrifying experience of divine anger and God-forsakenness.

This is the dark backdrop against which the restorative words of hope and promise sparkle. There is no escapist fantasy here; hope blossoms in the rocky ground of a very painful reality. The promises relativise the suffering by relegating it to a brief moment, a blip in the long sweep of God's everlasting love and unshakable covenant faithfulness, but they do not erase it. Still, there is a preponderance of relief and amazement, a strong sense that the hoped-for future joy is imminent.

The reading moves through three evocative images: the rejected wife reconciled to her husband; God's covenant with Noah and the whole earth; and a magnificent, bejewelled city. The references to God are intensely relational: your God, your creator, your husband, your redeemer. In each stanza there is the assurance that present fear, sadness and helplessness will give way to joy and celebration because of what God is about to do.

The Images of Isaiah 54 in the Light of the Old Testament

The first image is that of a rejected wife reconciled to her husband. The prophets often spoke of the covenant – the relationship between God and God's people – in terms of marriage. The comparison is a powerful one, bringing together the themes of love, faithfulness and mutual commitment. But the prophets frequently employ the trope to explore its shadow side, imaging the rage and devastation that accompany the hurt of betrayal and breakdown of relationship.

The prophet Hosea lived this experience in his own troubled marriage and his oracles project his complex emotions of love, anger and tenderness onto God. (See particularly Hosea chapters 1-3 and 11.) God is cast as the faithful husband and the sinning people are the unfaithful wife. Having said that, however, it is noteworthy that in this reading there is no apportioning of blame. We are not told why the wife was forsaken nor given a litany of the wife's sins, but only a glimpse of the anger from which God / the husband repents. God's power and greatness are stressed.

It is important to name the potential for abuse if this image is inappropriately invoked in interpersonal relationships. The implied passivity of the wife who is expected to be grateful to be taken back by a spouse who has recovered from his fierce anger should ring alarm bells, particularly in situations of domestic abuse. What this metaphor does do well is to capture a sense of anguish and forsakenness giving way to hope, and of God's determination to change sorrow into joy. The vulnerability of intimate relationships has the potential for deep hurt, but also for great joy when genuine reconciliation is achieved. Love's depth is made visible not in the honeymoon period but after the storm

Fourth Reading • Isaiah 54:5-14

when the relationship is healed and fully restored.

The next stanza references Noah and the perpetual covenant that God made with all creation after the Flood. We do not hear the story of Noah in the Liturgy of the Word at the Easter Vigil, but we have had the creation story of Genesis 1 where God forms and shapes the world into a life-giving space in which human beings and all living creatures can thrive. The story of Noah and the Flood as recounted in Genesis 6-9 is a story of un-creation and re-creation. God, first of all, removes the limits that keep the primeval waters in place so that the earth returns to a watery chaos. (Gen 7:11) Then God re-establishes the boundaries and rhythms that make life on earth possible and repeats the mandate to fill the earth with life. The words and images used in Genesis 8:1-9:3 to describe the end of the Flood and the creatures re-emerging from the ark to fill the earth with life strongly echo Genesis 1.

> The re-experiencing of the prophetic tradition – that is, the rehearing and respeaking of the texts with fresh contemporaneity – does not depend primarily upon critical and technical interpretive matters, but upon a capacity for imagination and intuition, coupled with courage, which dares to assert that these texts, concretely located and specifically addressed, can now be and must be concretely relocated and specifically readdressed as illuminating and revelatory in contemporary contexts.
>
> WALTER BRUEGGEMANN
> *Texts that Linger, Words that Explode*

Although we might associate Noah's Ark with a cutesy theme for a child's bedroom, the Flood narrative is actually a powerful, complex story in which chaos and destruction give way to life and immense hope. In the prequel to the story of Noah, God regrets that he has made humanity who have polluted the whole earth with their evil. 'And the LORD was sorry that he had made humankind on the earth, and it grieved him to his heart.' (Gen 6:6 NRSV)

These words name the primal existential fear: could God, the ground of our very existence, give up on the whole project? This is not just naming our fear of death; it is the terror of annihilation, of falling into the abyss of non-being. After the catastrophic Flood, which wipes out all of life apart from the little community huddled on the ark, the remnant re-emerge into a new world, a world which God promises to keep in existence. It is this promise that the poet-prophet names in Isaiah 54.

The promise is hugely encouraging because it is not predicated on humanity's ability to do better: it is made 'even though every inclination of their heart is toward evil'. (Gen 8:21) 'I establish my covenant with you, that never again shall all flesh be cut off by the waters of a flood, and never again shall there be a flood to destroy the earth. (Gen 9:11 NRSV)

The archetypal fear of non-being is named and then quelled, not buried or pushed aside. The sign of that covenant between God and every living creature on the earth is the rainbow. (Gen 9:12-16) The beauty of light revealed through the prism of water droplets when the clouds threaten is the assurance of God's faithfulness and continued commitment to God's world.

Our prophet reminds his hearers of this covenant so that when it looks like their world is ending – described here as earthquake rather than flood, with the mountains departing and the hills shaking – they can be assured of God's continued love and faithfulness. (54:10) The God who meets them is the God who re-establishes order out of the chaos and whose mercy transforms furious grief into steadfast love.

The final image of a hope-filled future in the form of a magnificent, peaceful city repeats this promise of reversal and renewal. The one to whom the words are spoken is 'a wretched creature, storm-tossed, disconsolate'. I imagine a dilapidated old boat in a raging sea, about to break up, very different from a city with firm foundations. The city is like something from a fairy-tale, built

Fourth Reading • Isaiah 54:5-14

upon dazzling red and blue gems with ruby battlements, crystal gates and set safely behind a wall of precious stones. (54:11-2)

Cities and societies, particularly ones which display such opulence, are usually built upon injustice. But this city is filled with righteousness. It is 'remote from oppression' not only because it is itself free, but it does not oppress others – surely that is what it means for it to be founded on integrity and taught by the Lord. It is prosperous and fruitful with nothing to fear. What a wonderful promise for the storm-tossed, disconsolate one.

Historical Context

These words were originally addressed to the people of God in exile in Babylonia, on the cusp of return and restoration. The story of the Exile is told concisely in 1 Chronicles 36:16, 19-23, which is the First Reading for the Fourth Sunday of Lent in Year B. God's people were unfaithful to the covenant, so God tirelessly sent them prophets to warn them and call them back.

But they ridiculed the messengers of God, they despised his words, they laughed at his prophets, until at last the wrath of the Lord rose so high against his people that there was no further remedy. Their enemies burned down the Temple of God, demolished the walls of Jerusalem, set fire to all its palaces, and destroyed everything of value in it. The survivors were deported by Nebuchadnezzar to Babylon; they were to serve him until the kingdom of Persia came to power.

The Persians who eventually defeated the Babylonians, had a dramatically different approach to securing their empire. They allowed exiled peoples to return to their homelands and to rebuild their lives and their temples, thereby encouraging loyalty and lessening the appeal of rebellion. It is around this time of regime change that the prophet declares his message of hope. In these international events of history as they will play out in their own lives, the people are to recognise the hand of God at work. God has not cast them off forever but is about to lead them home. The story of exile, of alienation and separation, of oppression and bondage, is about to become a recapitulation of the Exodus, a story of freedom, of restoration and return.

For the people of Jerusalem who ended up in exile, the horror of the destruction of their city and of God's Temple within it, the massacre of many of its inhabitants and the long forced march of the survivors to a foreign land felt like the wrath of God unleashed upon them. The prophets from the beginning linked the well-being of the people and their existence in the Promised Land with faithfulness to their covenant with God and interpreted famine, drought and military defeat as curses activated when the covenant was broken. So, to see the city and its Temple reduced to rubble and to be forced from their homeland either meant that God was too weak to withstand the enemy and their gods, or that God had finally turned God's back on them and rejected them.

The prophets among the people in exile worked hard to rekindle hope. Firstly, they reminded the people that their God was not a weak local deity who had been trampled by the gods of empire, but the powerful creator of the whole earth. In Isaiah 54, the people are reminded that God is 'your creator' and that 'the Holy One of Israel ... is called the God of the whole earth'. (54:5) Secondly, they address the question of whether the covenant has been irretrievably broken, in other words, whether the exile community are no longer the people of God. The answer of the exilic prophets is an emphatic *no*. God will not divorce the people but will take them back. Although the covenant originally made at Sinai had been conditional on the people's obedience, here God promises an unconditional covenant like God made with all of creation in the time of Noah: 'My love for you will never leave you and my covenant of peace with you will never be shaken.' (54:10)

Fourth Reading • Isaiah 54:5-14

New Testament Interpretation

In Galatians 4, St Paul draws upon the opening lines of this prophecy, omitted at the Easter Vigil, as part of an allegorical interpretation of the story of Hagar and Sarah. He writes of Sarah, quoting Isaiah 54:1: 'But the other woman corresponds to the Jerusalem above; she is free, and she is our mother. For it is written, "Rejoice, you childless one, you who bear no children, burst into song and shout, you who endure no birth pangs; for the children of the desolate woman are more numerous than the children of the one who is married".' (Gal 4:26-27)

St Paul is combining the first image of joyful reversal that the prophet-poet uses in Isaiah 54, the barren woman who becomes a mother, and the closing image of the glorious city, which he has interpreted as the Heavenly City. He reads this prophecy alongside the story of Hagar and Sarah and the two sons that they bear for Abraham. (Gen 16; 21:1-20).

The link between these passages is the childless woman becoming a mother. Abraham and Hagar's child, Ishmael, was not the child of the promise, an honour kept for Sarah's child, Isaac, who was born when she was long past childbearing age. This is not the place to attempt an explanation of St Paul's complex argument in Galatians, or of the convoluted relationship between Sarah, Hagar and Abraham. Suffice it to say that St Paul quotes the beginning of Isaiah 54 and alludes to its closing image to make the connection between 'the childless woman who has borne children' – whom he identifies with Sarah – and the Church. He thus reads Isaiah 54 as Christian Scripture, as a word spoken to and about the Church.

St Paul's interpretation of Isaiah 54 demonstrates how this song addressed to ancient Israel can be re-heard by Christians. The ancient words of comfort and assurance to God's people become words spoken to the Church, and in St Paul's reading it is in particular the Church gathered from the nations where room is made for those who were formerly outside the covenant. The joyous announcement in Isaiah 54 is amplified to broaden the scope of its recipients. The seeds of this generosity are found in the prophecy itself, again in the omitted first stanza where we read that the barren women is to 'enlarge the site of your tent, and let the curtains of your habitations be stretched out' to make room for more people. (54:2-3) Therefore, through the poem of Isaiah 54, heard during the Easter Vigil, we can hear the story of our salvation in Christ.

This is not the only time where words from the poem are quoted in the New Testament. In the Bread of Life Discourse in John 6, Jesus proclaims: 'It is written in the Prophets, "And they shall all be taught by God"'. (John 6:46) This is word-for-word the same as the Greek version of Isaiah 54:13. Here is another subtle invitation to hear the ancient words anew as Christian Scripture, as God's word to us in Christ in the context of the Eucharist, which is the theme of John 6.

A Typological Reading of Isaiah 54

St Paul's appropriation of Isaiah 54 alongside his allegorical reading of Sarah and Hagar already displays a typological reading of the Old Testament. A typological reading sees in Old Testament figures a *pre*figuring or anticipation of Christ and the Church. In other words, what we meet in the Old Testament is interpreted as a shadow of the realities disclosed in the New Testament. In the case of Isaiah 54, the promise of return from exile becomes the Christian fulfilment of salvation in Christ. The Exile speaks of our alienation from God which is overcome through the Paschal Mystery. Each image in turn can be taken as a type and heard as speaking of the reality or *antitype* of the Church. She is the bride, the one saved through water (Baptism) and the heavenly Jerusalem.

Fourth Reading • Isaiah 54:5-14

The Gospels speak of Jesus as the bridegroom because he is the one who woos the people back to the love and mercy of God. In Ephesians, St Paul likens the relationship between Christ and Church to that of husband and wife. (Eph 5:23-32) It is perhaps significant that the metaphor occurs to him in a letter where he has been stressing how in Christ those who were far away, outside the covenant, have been embraced and included: 'But now in Christ Jesus you who were once far off have been brought near by the blood of Christ.' (Eph 2:13)

It is not just 'Church as bride' that is in view in the first stanza of this Fourth Reading at the Easter Vigil, it is the alienated, exiled people

> What we should be primarily attentive to is the presence of Christ, who is teaching us himself. This is the point of reading the Scripture lessons near, and by the light of the Paschal Candle. The Old Testament is read but in the light of Christ, and indeed in the light of Christ who is present today.
>
> ADRIEN NOCENT, *The Liturgical Year*

without hope and without God in the world who are called, redeemed, embraced by the merciful God who takes pity on them. The image is of the Church as the community of the redeemed, those who have been reconciled to God.

The book of Revelation conflates the images of bride and heavenly city: 'And I saw the holy city, the new Jerusalem, coming down out of heaven from God, prepared as a bride adorned for her husband.' (Rev 21:2) The seer in Revelation goes on to describe 'the bride, the wife of the Lamb' (Rev 21:9) as a magnificent golden city with walls and gates of precious gems. This heavenly city is where God and God's people dwell together forever. It is an image of the Church triumphant, of the glories of heaven and the beatific vision, the consummation of salvation.

The typology of the images of bride and bejewelled city are straightforward enough, But what about Noah? Although the ark was taken as a type of the Church by the early Fathers,[1] it is not really the ark that is in view here but the renewed covenant with all of creation after the Flood. In the New Testament, Noah's family being kept safe through the Flood is seen as a type of Baptism: 'God waited patiently in the days of Noah while the ark was being built. In it only a few people, eight in all, were saved through water, and this water symbolizes Baptism that now saves you also – not the removal of dirt from the body but the pledge of a clear conscience toward God. It saves you by the Resurrection of Jesus Christ, who has gone into heaven and is at God's right hand – with angels, authorities and powers in submission to him.' (1 Peter 3:20-22)

The context within the Easter Vigil liturgy itself suggests an allusion to the sacrament of Baptism. The prayer for the Blessing of Baptismal Water evokes the waters of creation, flood, crossing of the sea, Baptism of Jesus and the water flowing from Jesus' pierced side. Here are the relevant words for Noah:

> O God, who by the outpouring of the flood foreshadowed regeneration, so that from the mystery of one and the same element of water would come an end to vice and a beginning of virtue.

Note how these words hold together both terror and hope, the destruction and the redemption that make up the story of the Flood. And so, read typologically, the promise of God's irrevocable love bestowed upon God's people is related to the sacraments of the Church, in this case, Baptism.

Heard typologically, this poem which promises redemption is the assurance of our salvation in Christ through the Church,

---

1. See for example Cyprian commenting on 1 Peter 3:18-21: 'The one ark of Noah was a type of the one Church,' in *Early Latin Theology*, ed. and trans. S. L. Greenslade, LCC 5 (Philadelphia: Westminster Press, 1956), 151.

which God calls into renewed relationship. The promise of God's grace communicated through the sacraments, is unshakable. By our Baptism we are enfolded in the steadfast love of God which will never be revoked. And we look forward to the final coming of the Kingdom of God, to the glorious future of full and final salvation when sorrow and death will be swallowed up in joy and life everlasting.

How are we to make sense, though, of those terrifying hints of God-forsakenness? Historically they named the experience of God's people when Jerusalem was destroyed, and they were exiled. But what is their place in the Christian story? Commenting on the words 'I did forsake you for a brief moment', John Calvin asserted:

> We are adopted by God in such a manner that we cannot be rejected by him on account of the treachery of men; for he is faithful, so that he will not cast off or abandon his people. What the Prophet says in this passage must therefore refer to our feelings and to outward appearance, because we seem to be rejected by God when we do not perceive his presence and protection. And it is necessary that we should thus feel God's wrath ... that we may know that we are justly chastised. But we must also perceive his mercy; and because it is infinite and eternal, we shall find that all afflictions in comparison of it are light and momentary.[2]

Calvin does not want the certainty of election to be shaken! I will not attempt my own theological explanation here because the prophet does not offer a theological treatise, but a poem. Isaiah 54 powerfully names a human experience and a deep existential fear, and it is on the level of poetry and story that he resolves it, as I will indicate below.

2. John Calvin, *Commentary on the book of the Prophet Isaiah*, vol. 4, trans. W. Pringle (Grand Rapids: Eerdmans 1948), 140.

A Liturgical Reading

The typological interpretation of Isaiah 54, given above, is one that engages the intellect and offers great hope. But in the context of the Easter Vigil itself, enfolded by the power of its liturgy, we hear this prophetic poem best when we hear it as both Christ's story and our own story. These words are proclaimed as we move from the disorientating silence of Holy Saturday to stand on the cusp of Easter Sunday with its glorious pronouncement of the Resurrection.

We hear Isaiah 54 in the context of our immersion in the Paschal Mystery, alongside other readings that recount the story of God's creating and redeeming work and juxtaposed with the rituals of baptismal initiation and Eucharistic Celebration. The Epistle reading helps us to make the links by describing Baptism as our participation in Christ's death and Resurrection. In Isaiah 54, God's Word resonates experientially with the Easter journey from devastation to amazement and assures us that we are included in this story of redemption.

In Christ's story, these words can be heard as God's reply to Jesus' cry of desolation from the cross on Good Friday: 'My God, my God, why have you forsaken me?' (Matt 27:46, Mark 15:34, quoting Ps 22:1). However we interpret what is going on theologically, this is the cry of one who experiences himself as abandoned by God in his hour of deepest need. That may resonate with moments of deep darkness in our own lives. The Easter story is immensely powerful precisely because it does not try to whitewash that suffering and terror, but acknowledges it, plumbs its depths, and speaks Resurrection into it. If Isaiah 54 echoes richly with our own story, it is because it names the fear of abandonment and opens the way for God's love and mercy to encounter us there.

Fourth Reading • Isaiah 54:5-14

Responsorial Psalm

The Psalm that follows this Fourth Reading has at its response: 'I will praise you Lord, you have rescued me.' Responsorial psalms are carefully chosen to give us a path into appropriating the reading for ourselves as the community of God's people. We do well to pay attention to its invitation. The response we are being invited to make is gratitude for our salvation. We are cued to recognise that Isaiah 54 has proclaimed that God is the redeemer, the one who rescues God's people.

The Psalm takes the theme of reversal and restoration that runs through Isaiah 54 to a whole new level by referring to being raised from the dead: 'O Lord, you have raised my soul from the dead, restored me to life from those who sink into the grave.' This is the wonder that we celebrate at Easter, the breath-taking salvation of God who brings life out of death. This is Jesus Christ's story, and it becomes our story.

The Psalm also echoes that dark and troubling note from the reading about God's anger but contains it within praise that the terror is over: the morning has come. As Isaiah 54 did, the Psalm relativises that dark place as a brief moment within a long lifespan, and not the final word: 'His anger lasts but a moment, his favour through life At night there are tears, but joy comes with the dawn.'

We are reminded that the Easter story is about God coming to the help of the crucified Christ, and coming to our help. The mourning of Good Friday and the grief of Holy Saturday give way to the joyous amazement of Easter Sunday. Death is swallowed up in Resurrection; darkness gives way to celebration.

Questions for Reflection or Discussion

This reading allows us to linger at the turning point where sorrow and forsakenness are about to give way to the joy of resurrection. Read it again, pausing from time to time to add in the words of the response to the Psalm, 'I will praise you, Lord, you have rescued me'. How does this affect how you experience this text?

How does this reading help you to participate in the paschal journey from devastation to amazement?

5

The Fountain and the Banquet
Fifth Reading • Isaiah 55:1-11

COLUMBA McCANN, O.S.B.

Introduction

The Fifth Reading of the Vigil is a wonderful text and the reader will need little commentary in order to find nourishment in it. I suggest therefore that the reader begin by reading the text prayerfully before looking for further insights in the lines that follow. As I go through the text I will also take time and space to point out echoes that can be heard from other parts of the Bible.

This approach follows the lines proposed by the Second Vatican Council, where the reader is encouraged not only to study the text in relation to its original context but also to take into account the content and unity of the whole of Scripture, as well as the tradition of the Church.[1] Even though there are many human authors involved in the Bible, sometimes even conflicting voices, there is, in the end, one divine Author who, through so many different human stutterings and stammerings, is trying to get through to us by every available means.

The eminent theologian Karl Barth made a distinction between the words on the page of the Bible and the Word of God itself. If I have understood him correctly, the Word of God is an event that happens right now. God speaks to me (or to us). Summarising Barth's ideas, the Italian Benedictine Luigi Gioia says:

1. Dogmatic Constitution on Divine Revelation *Dei Verbum*, 12.

The written words [Scripture] speak to me only if and as God himself speaks to me when I read or hear them (Word of God). Properly speaking, therefore, the Word of God is the event (or the action) whereby some human limited and fallible words become the medium or the occasion through which God addresses me, reveals himself to me, reconciles me to himself and establishes me in fellowship with all those who have been reached by this same address.[2]

In the Middle Ages, St Aelred of Rievaulx, speaking about the interpretation of passages in Isaiah, says that 'the "riddles of words" and the "figures of history" in the text are like walls; they contain and conceal Christ.'[3] The architects of Scripture have included grates and windows in the walls, so that we may know that Christ is hiding even in the obscure passages. How might Christ manifest himself to each of us in the reading of this passage? The Holy Spirit employs a variety of tactics. St Aelred says: 'The Spirit, who established [Scripture] with such prudence, also ordered it to be broad enough for countless senses, countless interpretations, of which he reveals some to one person, some to another'.

All of this means that hearing Old Testament readings in the Easter Vigil is not just tracing a history that somehow leads up to the proclamation of the Resurrection. All of the readings, from both Testaments, can be taken as a proclamation from the angel at the tomb: 'He is risen!' The readings are read in the light of the Paschal Candle, whose light shines across every page.

Eating and Drinking with God

By way of initial comment on the text, a word or two about the

2. Luigi Gioia, 'Word of God and Monasticism in Karl Barth', *The American Benedictine Review* 68 (2017): 424.
3. Aelred of Rievaulx, *De oneribus* 27:2

Fifth Reading • Isaiah 55:1-11

background may be in order. The book of Isaiah has multiple authorship. Its original source is indeed the prophet Isaiah himself, and much of the first 40 chapters reflect his preaching at a time when the monarchy in Judah was hugely in need of reform and was heading for destruction. Later disciples of Isaiah (we might call them the school of Isaiah) looked back to the original genius of the prophet and saw therein ideas which could be reinterpreted for later, quite different situations.

Thus, the prophecies which we have in chapters 40 to 55 are believed to reflect a later situation when the people are in exile. Building on the foundations of the prophet Isaiah, these later prophecies are largely a message of consolation and hope, promising a restoration of prosperity and indeed a return to their homeland. In fact, the first words of this section begin, 'Console, console my people'. (Isa 40:1) The fact that within the book of Isaiah itself the message of the prophet is being reinterpreted for new situations suggests that this approach to reading sacred Scripture is a dynamic built into the text itself. It is a way of reading that the authors expect of us. Our passage is a hope-filled *finale* which rounds off this 'book of consolation'.

'Oh, come to the water, all you who are thirsty; though you have no money, come! Buy corn without money, and eat, and, at no cost, wine and milk.' (55:1) These words were addressed initially to people who may indeed have suffered for lack of food and drink, either as the exiles in Babylon or the remnant who struggled to survive in a desolate homeland. Some of them may well have been hungry, thirsty and penniless.

Notice the poetic symmetry:

    Come, you *thirsty*   [A]
    you have no *money* [B]
    without *money*   [B]
    wine and *milk*   [A]

On a literal level, water, food and drink are part of the Promised Land, a land flowing with milk and honey. The offering of the first fruits of the harvest as prescribed in the book of Deuteronomy (Deut 26:1-11) makes clear the link between the produce of the land and the history of God's intervention in the lives of the people by recounting the Exodus and the settlement in the land.

Our text from Isaiah is God's promise of a return to their homeland. A return to good food is also a return to a prosperous homeland. But food speaks of more. The promise of an end to material want acts at the same time as a metaphor which draws the people into a recognition of deeper hungers and a more satisfying source of spiritual nourishment. This becomes more evident when we look at the biblical echoes of this text within the larger canon of Scripture.

> Christ is the book whose parchment is flesh and whose writing is the Father's Word. ... The greatest book is the incarnate Son.
>
> MEDIEVAL LITURGICAL COMMENTARY

In God's hands the simple things of the earth speak of greater mysteries. Back in the time of Moses at Mount Sinai the elders of Israel ate and drank in the Lord's presence when the Lord made a covenant with them. There is nothing like a meal to bond people together. At Sinai the bond was with God: 'They actually gazed on God and then ate and drank.' (Exod 24:11) An invitation to eat and drink becomes for us an invitation into a renewed covenant with God.

God's wisdom is also portrayed as setting out a feast and calling people to taste the flavour of God's ways: 'Come and eat my bread, drink the wine which I have drawn!' (Prov 9:5) Medieval authors, writing in Latin, liked to point out a connection between wisdom (*sapientia*) and taste (*sapor*). We are being invited to acquire a taste for God's wisdom today.

Jesus himself, the wisdom of God in the flesh, offers us the bread of his teaching and of his own life given for us: 'I am the bread of life. No one who comes to me will ever hunger; no one who believes in me will ever thirst.... The bread that I shall give is my flesh, for the life of the world.' (John 6:35, 51) References to Jesus' use of food and drink as a metaphor for shared life are scattered across the Gospels. Ultimately, this is about sharing in God's life. Think of the meal which Levi gives in his honour (Matt 9:10-17), the parable of the prodigal son (Luke 15:11-31), told because of complaints that 'this man welcomes sinners and eats with them' (Luke 15:3), the parable of the great banquet (Luke 14:15-24), the meals at Bethany (Luke 10:38-42; John 12:1-8), the feeding of the crowds mentioned in all the Gospels, the presence of food in those Resurrection accounts where Jesus is actually recognised in the breaking of bread (Luke 24:30, 35), where he eats fish (Luke 24:43) and even cooks it himself (John 21:9) and, most significantly, the Last Supper. Meals are his special way of sharing his life with us.

Those who are newly baptised at the Easter Vigil will eat and drink for the first time at the Eucharistic banquet. They will experience, with their risen Lord, all that he had sought to convey in word and action through his earthly table fellowship, and indeed far more, now that he is risen. Celebrating the Holy Eucharist in the light of Isaiah, we come to appreciate more the gift that is freely given to us in Christ, not something earned.

Living Water

'Come to the water!' In chapter 4 of John's Gospel, Jesus says to the Samaritan woman at the well: 'If you knew the gift of God and who is asking you for a drink, you would have asked him, and he would have given you living water.' (John 4:10) Speaking of the water in the well itself he says: 'Everyone who drinks this water will be thirsty again. But whoever drinks the water I give him will never thirst. Indeed, the water I give him will become in him a fount of water springing up to eternal life.' (John 4:13-14) If only we really knew now what is on offer!

Jesus himself was, no doubt, physically thirsty many times during his earthly life. In the Gospel according to John he is presented as thirsty when he goes to the well and meets the Samaritan woman, to whom he offers the water of eternal life. The next, and only other, time we see him thirsty is on the cross (John 19:28), after which, water streams from his pierced side. Speaking of the deeper significance of this, the Second Vatican Council said that 'it was from the side of Christ as he slept the sleep of death upon the Cross that there came forth the "wondrous sacrament of the whole Church"'.[4]

In chapter 7 of St John, we read that Jesus stood up and said in a loud voice: 'Let anyone who is thirsty come to me and drink.' (John 7:37) We are being invited to share, through the Holy Spirit, in Jesus' own life. Further, we can pray with the psalms: 'Like the deer that years for running streams, so, my soul is thirsting for you, my God' (Ps 42); and 'O God, you are my God, for you I long, for you my soul is thirsting. My body pines for you like a dry weary land without water'. (Ps 63)

The call to the water in our Reading is certainly not the first mention of water during the Easter Vigil. In the First Reading, the book of Genesis depicts the spirit hovering of the water; in the Third Reading, from the book of Exodus, the people are set free from slavery by passing through the waters of the sea. Later in the Vigil, the Seventh Reading from Ezekiel will promise cleansing waters, and the reading from the Letter to the Romans will speak of Baptism itself as a sharing in the death and Resurrection

---

4. Constitution on the Sacred Liturgy *Sacrosanctum Concilium* no. 5. See John 19:34.

of Jesus. Remember too that at the Easter Vigil, people all over the world are listening to these words as they wait to be baptised, about to come to the water, about to be fed at the table of the Holy Eucharist. And at the Vigil we will pray, having heard this reading, 'graciously increase the longing of your people'.

The Wrong Kind of Food

The Lord continues to speak through his prophet: 'Why spend money on what is not bread, your wages on what fails to satisfy?' (55:2) Notice the traditional Hebrew form of rhyme. While in English poetry rhyme happens when words and syllables sound similar though not exactly the same (mine, time, fine, spine), in Hebrew it works on the level of ideas. The same idea is restated in a slightly different manner: why spend money / your wages on what is not bread / on what fails to satisfy?

Jesus says: 'Do not work for food that perishes, but for food that endures to eternal life, which the Son of Man will give you.' (John 6:27) Looking for the wrong kind of food is a metaphor for misdirected desire on a much more general level. Isn't this the story of our lives? Hankering and straining after something, only to discover that it doesn't satisfy in the end.

In the Lenten preparation for the Paschal Triduum there is surely a connection here with the discipline of fasting from food or with other forms of abstinence. What is going on when we fast, or attempt to fast? Reading many of the classic authors, one generally finds an explanation that says that we deliberately experience physical hunger in order to become aware of spiritual hunger. That sounds good, but can remain on the level of theory. It becomes easier to appreciate if one thinks about comfort eating. (An experience that is familiar to many of us and not just in theory!) Is it not true that comfort eating is something we use as a mild anaesthetic? We use it to distract ourselves from the emptiness, the heartache, the sheer inner bankruptcy from which we hide. When we allow ourselves to actually experience the emptiness, then we are, in the words of the Beatitudes, 'poor in spirit', and therefore finally ready to experience the kingdom of heaven. We can fast from our food-anaesthetic in order to feel the more painful spiritual hunger that prepares us to experience, even now, something of the kingdom of heaven.

Listening to the Word That Nourishes

'Listen, listen to me, and you will have good things to eat and rich food to enjoy. Pay attention, come to me; listen and your soul will live.' (55:2-3) Here the Lord renews his invitation. What is new here is the explicit call to listen: to God's word – God's wisdom – which is nourishing and life-giving. 'Listen' is the first word of Israel's great creed, the *Shema*:

> Listen, Israel: The Lord our God is the one, the only Lord. You must love the Lord your God with all your heart, with all your soul, and with all your strength. Let the words I enjoin on you today stay in your heart. You shall tell them to your children, and keep on telling them, when you are sitting at home, when you are out and about, when you are lying down and when you are standing up; you must fasten them on your hand as a sign and on your forehead as a headband; you must write them on the doorposts of your house and on your gates. (Deut 6:4-9)

Listening to the word of God is a major, and lengthy, part of the Easter Vigil. The very first reading, from Genesis, displays the power of that word: 'God said … and so it was.' But the word takes on a different dynamism in each context. What ultimately is on offer in this text from Isaiah? What is the source of nourishment? What is the real basis of life at its best? I think we find it in the

Fifth Reading • Isaiah 55:1-11

next two lines of our Reading: 'With you I will make an everlasting covenant out of the favours promised to David.' (55:3) Other translations say: 'my steadfast, sure love for David' (NRSV); 'the sure mercies of David' (Septuagint); 'my everlasting mercies for David' (Vulgate).

The steadfast love of God for David and his promises for the future are now given to the people as a whole. Can we get inside this Davidic experience of being the recipient of a promise of steadfast, sure love, of sure mercies, of everlasting mercies? If we can, then we are opening up a rich store of nourishment that can sustain us. I think we can do this when we pray lines from the psalms which celebrate the legacy of God's love for King David: 'He will call to me "You are my Father: my God, and the rock of my salvation". I will ever maintain my loving kindness toward him: and my covenant with him shall stand firm' (Ps 89:26, 28). In Psalm 18, the king responds to God's loving kindness: 'I love you, O Lord my strength. O Lord my crag, my fortress and my deliverer, my God, the rock to which I come for refuge.' (Ps 18:1-2) In Jesus the Son of David, the divine promise finally reaches its goal: 'His throne shall be as the sun before me; like the moon that is established for ever and stands in the heavens for evermore.' (Ps 89:36-37)

> As soon as they come up from those sacred waters all present embrace them, greet them, kiss them, congratulate and rejoice with them, because those who before were slaves and prisoners have all at once become free men and sons who are invited to the royal table. For as soon as they come up from the font, they are led to the awesome table which is laden with all good things. They taste the body and blood of the Lord and become the dwelling place of the Spirit; since they have put on Christ, they go about appearing everywhere like angels on earth and shining as brightly as the rays of the sun.
>
> ST JOHN CHRYSOSTOM
> *Baptismal Catechesis*

As the candidates wait to be baptised at the Easter Vigil, they may indeed feel that they could not possibly share in such an exalted covenant of love with God, the love of God for King David, for Jesus the Son of David, but later that night they will actually drink from the cup: 'This is the chalice of my blood, the blood of the new and eternal covenant, which will be poured out for you and for many for the forgiveness of sins.' Come, all you who are thirsty, though you have no money come, eat and drink of the new covenant! Each baptised person is to taste for themselves what it is like to know God as Father, rock, strength, fortress, deliverer, shield in the way that Jesus himself does.

The prophet spoke to his poor, exiled, marginal people and promised that the Holy One of Israel would glorify them in a way that would speak to all nations. I wonder if he realised what he was saying, and how, through Jesus, the destiny of this little people, so often squeezed between the surrounding super-powers of Assyria, Babylon, Persia, Greece and Rome would finally explode into glory across the world because of the Cross and Resurrection of Jesus? The prayer that follows this Reading and its Psalm on Easter night says that God, 'by the preaching of [the] prophets, unveiled the mysteries of this present age'. The words of the prophet glow now with the light of the Paschal Candle.

God's Word Heralds Change and Brings about Transformation

Looking back with nostalgia, the people of Judah might have dreamt of their ruined temple, where God's name had made its home, where God could be found and addressed in prayer. But now even in exile, among the idols of the Babylonians, the prophet pointed out, God could be found anywhere, everywhere: 'Seek the Lord while he is still to be found, call to him while he is still near.' (55:6) God is always near!

Moving towards the second half of the text, we are being called to a whole new set of attitudes and priorities. God's ways are not ours. God's thoughts and projects and proposals are not ours. (55:8-9) Our way of seeing and planning has to change. St Paul might say that our mind has to be remade, or that we must put on the mind of Christ.

For a new convert awaiting Baptism this is the complete change of life involved in becoming a Christian; but for the already baptised it is also a call to a deep inner change, not just on the level of words and actions, but of mind and heart, thoughts, emotions, desires. This is what traditional monasticism would call guarding the mind and the heart; but it is for every baptised person, not just for monks and nuns. In the early centuries of the Church the candidates took off their clothes before Baptism before descending into the pool, as into a tomb. They re-emerged as from a womb and were given new garments. A whole new way of being in the world has to be discovered and lived.

God's ways are indeed different. The difference is as big as the distance between heaven and earth. But the prophet goes on to say that there is one thing that bridges the huge span between heaven and earth: just as the rain and the snow fall from heaven and water the earth to provide food and nourishment, so God's word, God's message and plan as it unfolds, can take root in our human nature and bring about transformation. (55:10-11) God is distant enough, different enough, to make a real difference, and near enough in Word and Spirit to transform us from within.

So, it seems that we are back to the call to listen. To listen to God's word is to be transformed, to be fed, to be nourished. Already at the Easter Vigil we will have heard of the creative power of God's word, as portrayed in the First Reading, from the first chapter of the book of Genesis: 'God said ... and it was so.' God's word not only creates the physical world but also creates history and moves it forward. When we listen to that word and make it our own we become collaborators with God in shaping history as it unfolds today. We do not live on bread alone, but on every word that comes from the mouth of God. This idea recurs like a refrain during the Lenten liturgy and finds an echo here in the Easter Vigil.

Praying in Response to the Reading

The Responsorial Psalm is like a two-way mirror: it is the word of God to us, but it is also, at God's inspiration, the prayer of the Church, our prayer. Through it God teaches us how to pray. It holds great liturgical and pastoral importance, because it fosters meditation on the word of God, and for this reason should be sung, or at least recited in a meditative way.

The Psalm paired with the Fifth Reading is one of those psalms not found in the book of Psalms itself but inserted rather into the book of the prophet Isaiah. The original context of the psalm is one of rescue from danger, as celebrated in the first two lines, which are omitted in this particular liturgy: 'I praise you, Lord, you have been angry with me but your anger is now appeased and you have comforted me.' (12:1) The Psalm, as it stands in the liturgy, takes on a particular eloquence when prayed in the minds and hearts of those preparing to be baptised and also, by extension, by those of us who seek a renewal of the grace of Baptism.

Notice the repeated reference to being saved by God. 'Truly God is my salvation.' 'He became my Saviour.' 'With joy you will draw water from the wells of salvation.' A new vista, only hinted at in the reading, opens up in the psalm – the strength and might of God. 'The Lord is my strength, my song.' 'Make his mighty deeds known to the peoples.' 'He has done glorious deeds.' The Psalm is imbued with a sense of God's greatness. 'Declare the greatness of his name.' 'Great in your midst is the Holy One of Israel.'

Fifth Reading • Isaiah 55:1-11

This final title given to the Lord, the 'Holy One of Israel' recurs like a refrain (19 times) in passages of Isaiah. Indeed, in his original call the prophet Isaiah was seared by the experience of heavenly beings crying out in the temple 'Holy! Holy! Holy!' This acclamation will be taken up again in the Eucharistic Prayer of the Vigil.

Coupled with the greatness of the Lord is his merciful presence among his people. The 'name' of the Lord is a reverent way referring to his self-revelation. We cannot see God and live, but his name is present among us. The people of Zion were those who lived around the place of God's name *par excellence*, the temple of Jerusalem. Here they are invited to celebrate the greatness of the presence of the Holy One among them.

The mighty deeds of the Lord and the greatness of his presence in the new people of Zion (the gathered liturgical assembly) are celebrated on this holy night, not only in relation to the raising of Jesus from the dead but also, flowing from this, in the interior resurrection that takes place in the minds, hearts and lives of those who, through Baptism, place their faith in him. 'I trust, I shall not fear.' The mighty deeds of the Lord unfold on this very night among those who gather.

Hallowed Be Thy Name

Speaking of the Old and New Testaments, the Second Vatican Council, drawing on St Augustine, said that 'God, the inspirer and author of the books of both Testaments, in his wisdom has so brought it about that the New should be hidden in the Old and that the Old should be made manifest in the New'.[5] In the Easter Vigil, the Old and New Testaments are not only proclaimed; they are celebrated sacramentally in Baptism and Eucharist, and those who are baptised will pray the Our Father with the whole

---

5. Dogmatic Constitution on Divine Revelation *Dei Verbum* no. 16.

assembly in preparation for receiving the Holy Eucharist. In the Lord's Prayer, the spirit of the newly-baptised cries out 'Abba, Father!' bringing into the full light of Christian prayer the sentiments already proclaimed in the reading and its accompanying psalm. The newness of life in Christ shines out already in these texts of the old covenant.

Questions for Reflection or Discussion

How can you hear the angel's proclamation that 'He is risen!' in the words of this reading?

How do the themes of listening, being transformed, being fed and being nourished tie in with the overarching theme of the Easter Vigil?

6

Return to the Fountain of Wisdom

Sixth Reading • Baruch 3:9-15,32–4:4

SUSAN DOCHERTY

Introduction

The Sixth Reading is probably the one most likely to be omitted from the Easter Vigil, considered marginal or non-essential to the liturgy because it does not seem to address directly the Paschal themes of Resurrection and redemption. It stands out as different from the other prescribed readings because, although attributed to the prophet Baruch, its form and content are closer to the genre of wisdom (as found in, for example, the books of Job or Ben Sira) than to prophecy. It is also the only passage drawn from the collection of writings accepted as Scripture by the Roman Catholic and Orthodox Churches, but not included in Protestant or Jewish Bibles, that is from the deutero-canonical literature. The book of Baruch as a whole is not particularly well-known, as it is seldom used in any liturgical context, and is appealed to as an authoritative source for doctrine only very infrequently.

It is perhaps, surprising, then, that this text should have been chosen for proclamation at the most solemn Christian festival of the year, alongside extracts from the major prophets Isaiah and Ezekiel, and following the narration of such significant episodes as the creation and the Exodus. In fact, however, as this chapter will explore, it puts forward an understanding of God's constant presence with people which adds a unique theological dimension to the Easter Liturgy of the Word and has ongoing relevance for worshippers in their daily lives.

Background and Context: The Book of Baruch

The author of this work is unknown, as is the specific historical context in which it was produced. It is associated with Baruch, a figure who appears several times in the book of Jeremiah (*e.g.*, chapters 32, 36, 43 and 45) as the scribe and companion of the prophet. Jeremiah was active in one of the most turbulent periods recorded in the Bible, the time leading up to and immediately following the decisive defeat of the Kingdom of Judah by the forces of King Nebuchadnezzar in 587 BCE, and the consequent forced removal of large sections of the population to Babylonia (also known as Chaldea). The narrative setting of this text, then, is among these early Jewish exiles, as they try to make sense of the catastrophe which has befallen them: 'These are the words of the book which Baruch the son of Neraiah ... wrote in Babylon, in the fifth year, on the seventh day of the month, at the time when the Chaldeans took Jerusalem and burned it with fire.' (Bar 1:1-2) It is one of several biblical and deutero-canonical writings connected by name or by theme to the book of Jeremiah, including Lamentations and the Epistle of Jeremiah. Indeed, when quoting from Baruch, some of the early Church fathers actually attributed its words directly to Jeremiah, indicating that it was regarded as a sort of extension of the main collection of his prophetic oracles.[1]

The close relationship between the two works may help to explain the selection of this passage for the Vigil. It stands where a

---

1. A clear example of this can be seen in *Against Heresies*, written by Irenaeus of Lyons in the late second century CE. He prefaces a lengthy quotation from Baruch 4:36-5:9 with the phrase 'And Jeremiah the prophet has pointed out...'.

Sixth Reading • Baruch 3:9-15. 32–4:4

reading from Jeremiah might be expected, sandwiched by the two other great exilic and early post-exilic prophets, Isaiah and Ezekiel. The Baruch who knew Jeremiah is not the actual author of this book, however, as it was composed much later, probably in stages during the second century BCE, and perhaps in Greek rather than Hebrew.[2] There are no clear indications in the text itself of its date or historical circumstances, so commentators have to consider evidence such as any sign of the author's knowledge of books which can be dated (such as Ben Sira), or how far the allusions to other scriptural passages within Baruch seem to reflect the Greek translation of the Bible (known as the Septuagint), which was not begun before the third century BCE. Baruch is not even mentioned again after the introductory verses (1:1-9), so it seems very likely that the use of his name is a device designed to link this later book with both an authoritative biblical work in Jeremiah, and with a major episode in Israel's history, the exile.

In a culture which greatly valued tradition and the wisdom of the ancients, this technique of attributing new writings to a highly-regarded figure of the past, or pseudepigraphy, was widespread. It continued to be employed by the early Christians, as exemplified by the association with the apostle Paul of letters composed after his death, such as 1 Timothy.

A significant number of later works were ascribed to Baruch, especially in the aftermath of the destruction of Jerusalem by the Romans in 70 CE, an event with obvious analogies to the defeat by the Babylonians 600 years earlier. A text composed at the very end of the first century of the Christian era, known as 2 Baruch, is a response to this later disaster, for example, and it, in turn, influenced subsequent writings, such as 3 Baruch and 4 Baruch.

---

2. A range of dates has been suggested by commentators, spanning the second century BCE to the second century CE. For a concise summary of the arguments see S. A. Adams, *Baruch and the Epistle of Jeremiah: A Commentary Based on the Texts in Codex Vaticanus* (Leiden: Brill, 2014), 4-6.

The religions of Judaism and Christianity have always been shaped by this process of on-going reflection on the Scriptures, and by the creative re-use of older tradition. The whole Easter Vigil involves such an active and participatory remembering of the story of salvation history, from creation, through exile, right up to the death and Resurrection of Jesus.

Interestingly, some commentators think that the book of Baruch may itself have been compiled for use as a liturgy, with the overarching theme of exile and redemption, as, following the narrative introduction (1:1-14), it contains a long communal confession of sin (1:15-3:8); then moves to a divine response to this prayer, a call for a return to faithfulness to the Law, from which the Easter Vigil reading is taken (3:9-4:4); and ends with a promise of forgiveness and restoration for Israel (4:5-5:9), inspired by the consoling words of Isaiah chapters 40-55: 'Look toward the east, O Jerusalem, and see the joy that is coming to you from God! Behold, your sons are coming, whom you sent away; they are coming, gathered from east and west, at the word of the Holy One, rejoicing in the glory of God.' (4:36-37)[3]

Major Themes:
Wisdom, Law and Life

The central section of the book of Baruch is clearly marked as a new unit by a change of speaker. Following the prayer of the people of Israel (1:15–3:8), this reading introduces God's own words, addressing the community directly in the first person through the prophet. The style also differs markedly from what has gone be-

3. For this theory of an original liturgical use, see especially M. A. Wes, 'Mourning Becomes Jerusalem: Josephus, Jesus the Son of Ananias, and the Book of Baruch (1 Baruch)', in *Sacred History and Sacred Texts in Early Judaism: A Symposium in Honour of A. S. van der Woude*, eds. J. N. Bremmer and F. García Martínez (Kampen: Kok Pharos Publishing House, 1992), 119–150.

Sixth Reading • Baruch 3:9-15. 32–4:4

fore, as a poetic, psalm-like form is adopted, and considerable use is made of imperatives (*e.g.*, 'listen', 'hear', 'learn' in 3:9, and 'turn back', 'seize', 'make your way' in 4:2). Both features are typical of the wisdom literature. These divine words are presented as a message for a people in exile, just like those in the Fourth, Fifth and Seventh Readings, from Isaiah and Ezekiel. The original audience of the book of Baruch are being invited, then, to associate themselves with the experience of their ancestors, crushed by the Babylonians and banished to a foreign land.

> Blessed are you, Lord our God, King of the universe, who has given us the Torah of truth and planted eternal life within us. Blessed are you Lord, who gives the Torah.
>
> JEWISH PRAYER
> AFTER READING FROM THE TORAH

Over the course of the following centuries, this national humiliation became the paradigm for every disaster to afflict the people of Israel. Jewish leaders and teachers returned to these events again and again, as they tried to make sense of later catastrophes, and to reconcile them with what they believed about God's goodness and mercy, and with the promises of God's faithfulness to Israel made in the covenant.

The inclusion of this reading in the Paschal liturgy is a powerful reminder that Christians, too, are rooted in this story of Israel, which includes instances of disobedience to God, defeats and all kinds of difficulties, as well as times of joy and liberation, like the Exodus. The Easter congregation are, therefore, repeatedly and explicitly addressed in this reading as part of the people of Israel or Jacob: 'Listen, Israel, to commands that bring life'; (3:9) 'Turn back, Jacob, seize her'; (4:2) 'Israel, blessed are we; what pleases God has been revealed to us'. (4:2-4). They are reminded in this text, too, that it is not only Jesus, but also Israel, who is called God's servant and well-beloved. (3:36).

This shared heritage with Judaism has sometimes been underplayed in Christian theology, but a deeper appreciation of it is vital for understanding Christian origins and for making progress in inter-faith dialogue. Especially since the Second Vatican Council, the teaching of the Catholic Church has stressed that Christians have not replaced or superseded the Jewish people in God's covenant or plans for salvation, since 'the gifts and the call of God are irrevocable'. (Rom 11:29)[4] Rather, Christians believe that they are now able to share in the words of invitation, forgiveness and love first addressed to Israel and preserved in the Scriptures.

This relationship is a theme of the wider Triduum liturgy, as illustrated by the sixth of the Solemn Intercessions in the celebration of Jesus' Passion on Good Friday: 'Let us pray also for the Jewish people, to whom God spoke first, that he may grant them to advance in love of his name and in faithfulness to his covenant.'

The imagery employed at the start of the Sixth Reading to characterise the experience of exile is stark. (3:10-11). The people are pictured as growing old in a foreign country, a description suggestive of both the length of time that their exile has lasted, and of a sense of despair that it may not end in their lifetime, so that they may never see their own homes again. The land in which they now live is said to be 'alien', and a place of death, comparable to the shadowy underworld of *Sheol*, which the spirits of the departed were thought to inhabit. The exiles feel themselves to be unclean or defiled, perhaps because of their burden of guilt for the sin which they believed had contributed to their current situation, or because they cannot carry out the traditional cleansing rituals and Temple sacrifices outside Israel.

The reference to their 'sharing defilement with the dead' (3:10) may even be a subtle evocation of the siege conditions endured in the Babylonian war, which had compelled some to turn in des-

---

4. Particularly significant Vatican documents are *Nostra Aetate* (1965) and *The Jewish People and Their Sacred Scriptures in the Christian Bible* (2001).

Sixth Reading • Baruch 3:9-15, 32–4:4

peration to cannibalism in order to survive: 'Under the whole of heaven there has not been done the like of what he has done in Jerusalem ... that we should eat, the one the flesh of his son and another the flesh of his daughter.' (2:2-3) It may also be a metaphor for idolatry, since following other gods is often associated in the Scriptures with death, or described as a defilement. Jeremiah, for example, asks the people of his time: 'How can you say, "I am not defiled. I have not gone after the Baals"?' (Jer 2:23) The author of the Book of Wisdom instructs his readers that, 'miserable, with their hopes set on dead things, are the men who give the name "gods" to the works of men's hands'. (Wis 3:10)

Although Baruch's original audience were not the first generation of exiles, they either still felt its effects in their community and religious life, or were recalling that experience, whether in the context of a liturgy, or during new times of danger and difficulty. Baruch declares that God speaks directly into this situation of suffering and distress in answer to their prayer.

People today can continue to draw hope from this affirmation that they are never separated from the blessings or revelation of God, either geographically or metaphorically, no matter what pain they are going through, how distant from God they feel, or how marginalised they consider their traditions to be within a dominant but 'alien' culture. The whole Easter Vigil liturgy takes contemporary worshippers deep into this figurative experience of exile, in order to dramatically re-enact the liberation from it which Christians believe is offered through the death and Resurrection of Jesus.

So Ezekiel, for example, forcefully reminds his hearers of their sin which contributed to their rout by the Babylonian forces. Like Baruch, he uses the language of 'defilement', but holds out also the promise of future forgiveness, and a return to the land of Israel: 'I then discharged my fury at them because of the blood they shed in their land and the idols with which they defiled it. I scattered them among the nations and dispersed them in foreign countries.... But ... I am going to take you from among the nations and gather you together from all the foreign countries, and bring you home to your own land.' (Ezek 36:18-19, 24).

In the Vigil's New Testament reading from Romans, this hope is seen to be fulfilled in Paul's promise that human slavery to sin and exile from God can be overcome in the new life offered through Baptism into Christ's death. (Rom 6:3-9)

Baruch is dealing with the same issues of sin and alienation from God among his community. His solution is to call them to return to faithfulness to the Mosaic Law. His claims that this law gives life (3:1, 14), peace (3:13, 14), strength (3:14), and light (3:14) offer a powerful rhetorical contrast to his earlier account of the people's experience of death and despair.

Some modern readers may struggle with the notion that 'law' is a life-giving and illuminating gift from God, since the term can carry with it overtones of rigidity and restrictions to freedom, or be perceived as a standard which it is virtually impossible to live up to in today's complex world. Such negative connotations are not part of the traditional Jewish understanding of the Law or *Torah*, however. Rather, Jews believe that it encompasses more than simply rules, so that it provides an insight into the divine nature, connects people with God, and enables them to relate their religion to every aspect of life. They feel privileged to have received it, therefore, and give thanks for this blessing regularly in prayer.

This positive attitude to the Law is brought out clearly in the psalm paired with the Sixth Reading: 'The precepts of the Lord... gladden the heart ... The decrees of the Lord ... are more to be desired than gold, than the purest of gold, and sweeter are they than honey, than honey from the comb.' (Ps 19:8-10) The importance of the Law for future salvation is highlighted also in some

Sixth Reading • Baruch 3:9-15. 32–4:4

of the other readings from the prophets at the Vigil. Ezekiel, for example, anticipates a time when God will 'put my spirit in you, and make you keep my laws and sincerely respect my observances'. (Ezek 36:27)

The contemporary relevance of this law is heightened by the fact that it is understood in the Scriptures as something which promotes the welfare not of individuals, but of the whole community. Baruch's emphasis on it is a response to a *communal* prayer in the first part of the book, and his message is addressed to the people collectively, using plural imperatives and pronouns. The Law offers life to all members of society, therefore, especially those most in need of God's justice, like the poor, orphans and refugees, who are placed at the centre of God's commandments: 'When you reap your harvest in your field, and have forgotten a sheaf in the field, you shall not go back to get it; it shall be for the sojourner, the fatherless, and the widow.' (Deut. 24:19)

> The search for a just and righteous wisdom for life is one of the basic religious attitudes of human beings. This may be the commonality between religions, as almost all religions recommend searching sincerely for the way to wisdom
>
> KYUNG-SOOK LEE
> *Wisdom Commentary Series 31*

This reading illustrates a further development in Jewish thought about the Law which became important in the early centuries BCE – its identification with divine wisdom. According to Baruch, Israel's exile has come about because they 'have forsaken the fountain of wisdom'. (3:12) He then explains that this wisdom is in fact 'the book of the commandments of God, the law that stands for ever'. (4:1) As Israel's long-standing wisdom tradition, attested in books like Proverbs, evolved, it came first to personify wisdom as a feminine attribute of God, and then to equate this divine wisdom with the *Torah*. A classic example of this move is found in Ben Sira, where, after a lengthy poem praising heavenly wisdom, and describing her role in creation, the scribe states: 'All this is the book of the covenant of the Most High God, the law which Moses commanded us.' (Sir 24:23)[5]

The early Church fathers built on this idea, and identified Christ with the divine wisdom, an understanding which is hinted at in New Testament passages like the prologue to the Fourth Gospel: 'And the word became flesh and dwelt among us, full of grace and truth.' (John 1:14) A particular verse from this Baruch passage became an important plank of scriptural support for the incarnation, cited in this context by, for instance, Thomas Aquinas in his *Summa Theologiae* (III, 4, 4): 'so causing her to appear on earth and move among men.' (3:37) This reception history helps to explain the selection of this reading for the Easter Vigil liturgy, and Baruch's confidence that God is present with people in their everyday lives adds to the hopefulness of the Easter message.

The image of wisdom as being like a water-source or 'fountain' (3:12) is another important link between this passage and the main themes of the Vigil. Water serves as a powerful symbol of cleansing and redemption for the prophets Isaiah and Ezekiel in the Fifth and Seventh Readings: 'Oh, come to the water all you who are thirsty.' (Isa 55:1) 'I shall pour clean water over you and you will be cleansed.' (Ezek 36:25) It also calls to mind Jesus' offering of himself as living water to the Samaritan woman (John 4:13-14) and, above all, it evokes the baptismal water which will be blessed as the centre-piece of the Paschal celebration.

Baruch's conclusion that true wisdom lies only with God, and in the Law which God has communicated to the people of Israel, is arrived at in response to a rhetorical question, a literary convention widely employed in the wisdom literature: 'But who

---

5. For a fairly recent full-length study of this development, see Alice M. Sinnott, *The Personification of Wisdom* (Aldershot: Ashgate, 2005).

has found out where she [wisdom] lives, who has entered her treasure house?' (3:15)

The prescribed reading is a shortened form of this section of Baruch, however, and the omitted verses (3:16-31) include a series of negative answers to this question. These intervening lines spell out that wisdom is not to be found in the places where many people look for it, such as among the powerful, ruling classes, or in amassing wealth. Nor do those renowned for their learning and dedicated to the search for knowledge always find it, as Paul would later tell the Christians in Corinth: 'Has not God made foolish the wisdom of the world?... For the foolishness of God is wiser than men.' (1 Cor 1:20-25) The Lectionary's concentration at this point only on the positive answer serves to direct the focus of the congregation as quickly as possible on to Jesus, understood in the light of the Resurrection as the divine wisdom incarnate, and the bringer of life and light to humanity.[6]

The Re-Use of Older Scripture in the Book of Baruch

The books of the Bible are full of allusions and connections to one another, as prophets and teachers continued to reflect on these authoritative sources and draw out their ongoing relevance for new situations. As we have seen, Baruch is no exception to this practice, and it is important to recognise both how deeply rooted this reading is in scriptural language and thought, and how creatively it adapts specific traditions. Two other texts, in particular, appear to have been influential in shaping this section of the book – chapter 28 of Job, and Deuteronomy, especially

---

6. For a similar view, and a further detailed discussion of this reading, see Nuria Caldach-Benages, 'The Baruch Reading at the Easter Vigil (Baruch 3:9-15; 3:32-4:4)', in *Studies on Baruch: Composition, Literary Relations and Reception*, ed. S. A. Adams (Berlin: de Gruyter, 2016), 153-170.

chapters 4 and 30.

The Job passage sets out to answer a question similar to that raised by Baruch: 'Where shall wisdom be found? And where is the place of understanding?' (Job 28:12) This author draws the same conclusion that true wisdom lies only in God, and he, too, specifically rejects the view that it is to be found in riches: 'It cannot be gotten for gold ... God understands the way to it, and he knows its place.' (Job 28:15, 23). Like Baruch, he also regards this wisdom not as a merely theoretical concept, but as a reality which is made manifest in concrete acts of justice in everyday life: 'The fear of the Lord, that is wisdom; and to depart from evil is understanding.' (Job 28:28)

Two interesting and inter-related differences emerge, however, when Job 28 and Baruch 3 are closely compared. First, Job's question is about the *place* where wisdom is to be found, while Baruch focuses more on the *person* seeking wisdom, and so asks: 'who has found out where she lives, who has entered her treasure house?' (3:15). Second, Job understands wisdom as essentially a divine attribute, and so declares that it cannot be discovered on earth: 'Man does not know the way to it, and it is not found in the land of the living.' (Job 28:13) The identification, over time, of wisdom with the Jewish Law, discussed above, enabled later teachers to take a different view of its accessibility. Baruch could respond positively to the needs of his community, therefore, and reassure them that God's presence and wisdom is worth seeking out, because it is available to people in every geographical location and in even the most difficult of circumstances.

Baruch also draws on the book of Deuteronomy to inform his teaching here. In this account of the giving of the commandments, Moses is presented as encouraging the Israelites to keep them because doing so will secure for them life in the land of Canaan: 'And now, O Israel, give heed to the statutes and the ordinances which I teach you, and do them; that you may live, and go in and take possession of the land which the Lord, the God of your fathers gives you.' (Deut 4:1) Baruch shares this Deuteronomic confidence that the life-giving laws have been made known and can be followed, bringing people very near to God, wherever they find themselves.

Conclusion

The Sixth Reading coheres fully with the wider Easter Vigil Liturgy of the Word, then, and admirably complements its major themes. It forms part of the whole movement of these readings through the key events of salvation history, from creation, by way of the lives of the patriarchs and the Exodus, to the time of the Babylonian exile, one of the lowest points in Israel's story. Like Isaiah and Ezekiel, Baruch reflects on this catastrophe in the light of other scriptural texts, and is able to draw out from it a message of hope for the people of his own later times. He emphasises God's ability to speak even in situations of pain and disaster, even outside the land of Israel, and even to people overwhelmed by a burden of sin and suffering.

This reading addresses the contemporary Christian congregation as 'Israel', thereby providing a vivid reminder that Jews and Christians share in one scriptural narrative of God's actions and redeeming love, and are united by a common history and Law. For Baruch, this Law is life-giving because it is God's way of being ever-present to people and, if followed, can secure the welfare of society as a whole. His poignant description of God's wisdom as 'moving among men' (3:37) resonates with the central Christian message of the incarnation. In bringing together all three scriptural traditions, Law, prophecy and wisdom, to point to the hope and light offered in God's word, as spoken both in the ancient

Scriptures of Israel and in the person of Jesus, Baruch serves as a unique bridge from the Old Testament into the New.

Questions for Reflection or Discussion

What difference does an understanding of the close connections between Christianity and Judaism make to your faith?

How, or through whom, is God's wisdom made visible in your life today?

7

Water, Heart and Spirit

Seventh Reading • Ezekiel 36:16-28

MARTIN BROWNE, O.S.B.

Introduction

According to the Church's official instruction on the celebration of Easter, the role of the readings at the Paschal Vigil is to 'give the account of the outstanding deeds of the history of salvation'. The same document goes on to explain:

> The restored order for the Vigil has seven readings from the Old Testament, chosen from the law and the prophets, which are everywhere in use according to the most ancient tradition of East and West; and two readings from the New Testament, namely, from the apostles and from the Gospel. Thus, the Church, 'beginning with Moses and all the prophets', explains Christ's Paschal Mystery.[1]

While the claim that the same Vigil readings have been used across the entire Church throughout history is attractive, it is not entirely true. We have records of the readings used in various liturgical traditions from the fifth century onwards, and while some of the current readings have indeed been part of the Vigil since then or before, the reading from chapter 36 of the book of the prophet Ezekiel was included in the Paschal Vigil for the

---

1. *Paschale Solemnitatis,* Congregation for Divine Worship and Discipline of the Sacraments (1988), no. 85.

very first time in 1970. Its inclusion indicates a renewal of the baptismal understanding of the Vigil that has flourished in the Church since the Second Vatican Council.

To suggest that a text that dates from centuries before the time of Jesus should be understood as referring in some way to Baptism may seem a bit strange. It is worth looking again at that paragraph from the Church's document about the Triduum. It says of the readings: 'thus, the Church ... explains Christ's Paschal Mystery'. That is an extraordinary statement, and one which we would be foolish to overlook. In reading it, it is good to recall that the Lord himself speaks when we read the Scriptures in the liturgical assembly.

Thus the readings are more proclamations or revelations than mere readings of pieces of text. The readings of the Easter Vigil have been assembled by the Church in order to *explain* the Paschal Mystery of Christ, its Head. This suggests that we are to listen to them so as to hear and understand what Jesus has done for humankind by his Passion and his Passover – his suffering, his death on the Cross and his Resurrection to new life. Baptism is our gateway to participation in that Paschal Mystery, and so, regardless of whether the sacraments of initiation are conferred at a particular celebration of the Vigil or not, the Easter Vigil always has a strong baptismal character.

What Had Become Old Is Made New

Rather than beginning with an examination of the reading itself, it would be helpful to look first at the prayer that follows the reading and its psalm. The reading is but one part of the richest and most complex liturgical experience of the entire Church year and that context, in which the various readings, prayers, actions and gestures interpret and illuminate each other, is hugely important.

In the case of the Ezekiel reading there are two options from

Seventh Reading • Ezekiel 36:16-28

which the prayer after the Responsorial Psalm may be chosen. The first is quite poetic, the second a bit more prosaic. But it says something important about the function of the readings at the Vigil, reinforcing the idea that they are intended to *explain* the paschal mystery. It prays that 'we may comprehend your mercy, so that the gifts we receive from you this night may confirm our hope of the gifts to come'. As a prayer it expresses elegantly what a worshipper's intention ought to be as he or she prepares to keep vigil during the holy night: that our extended period of listening may help us to understand the mercy and loving-kindness of God throughout all of human history; and that the holy gifts received in the Eucharist may keep us strong in our faith and confident of the promise of eternal life with God, beyond human history.

The other prayer is more elaborate and has a poetic and cosmic sweep. It has much clearer echoes of the reading that it follows, but also, like the alternative prayer, sums up the overarching thrust of the entire collection of Old Testament proclamations at the Vigil. It asks God to 'look with favour on the wondrous mystery of the whole Church and serenely accomplish the work of human salvation', praying that 'the whole world [may] know and see that what was cast down is raised up, what had become old is made new, and all things are restored to integrity through Christ, just as by him they came into being'.

This prayer can be a real help in appreciating what we celebrate in the Easter Vigil. It reminds us that the Paschal Mystery is not small or limited. It is not a favour or an indulgence for some small group or elite sect. It is about God healing and saving the whole of creation. Nor is it just a celebration of the restoration to life of the human body of Jesus of Nazareth. Rather, it is the saving of the world and the raising up of a fallen creation.

The first Old Testament reading spoke of the creation of the universe, and this final Old Testament reading tells of its restoration, its re-creation. While Christians have long discerned the presence and action of Christ in the Creation story, this prayer proclaims it explicitly when it prays that 'the whole world [may] know and see that ... all things are restored to integrity through Christ, just as by him they came into being'. Christ was there at the first beginning of the world, because he is the Eternal Son of the Father, and now, through his Paschal Mystery, he has effected a new beginning. And he will be there on the last day, when God makes all things new and there is a new heaven and a new earth.

> Our God is not a remote God, intangible in his blessedness. Our God has a heart. Indeed, he has a heart of flesh; he was made flesh precisely to be able to suffer with us and to be with us in our suffering. He was made man to give us a heart of flesh and to reawaken within us love for the suffering, for the destitute. Let us pray to the Lord that he will truly give us a heart of flesh, that he will make us messengers of his love not only with words, but with our entire life.
>
> BENEDICT XVI,
> Via Crucis, Good Friday 2007

The word 'new' is key here. It is a key word in this reading from Ezekiel too, even though it only appears twice in the passage – 'new heart' and 'new spirit'. (Ezek 36:26) For what is the Resurrection of the Lord Jesus about if not new life – life that is brand new, fresh and youthful, and of a nature entirely unknown until now? It is about the new life not just of Christ's physical body, but the new life that he opened up for all of creation by his sacrificial offering of himself to the Father. The Resurrection is about restoring what was lost through sin. It is about the redemption of slaves, freeing them – us – from bondage to sin. As the deacon or cantor sings in the *Exsultet*, 'our birth would have been no gain, had we not been redeemed.... O love, O charity beyond all telling, to ransom a slave you gave away your Son!' God's love and charity beyond all telling is what

Seventh Reading • Ezekiel 36:16-28

the Paschal Mystery is about. And at its heart, the love and charity of God beyond all telling is what creation is about. From the beginning of time, God has been pouring himself out in love. The very nature of God is to give of himself out of love. That is the context in which Ezekiel 36:16-28 is proclaimed at the Easter Vigil.

Exile and Restoration

But even with all of this contextualisation, the reading is still not an easy text to grasp without some historical background. As we read the text we notice that there are several references to scattering, exile, and foreign countries. These are important. Ezekiel was writing to a people who were in exile. They were not free. He was a priest, but the people whom he was addressing in this prophecy no longer had access to the Temple for their worship and sacrifices. This was the period in Israel's history known as the 'Babylonian Captivity'.

In the seventh century BCE, Babylon came to increasing prominence in its region, and largely overthrew the Assyrian Empire, to which it had previously been subject. As often happens with superpowers, even to this day in the political realm, Egypt grew nervous at the increase of Babylonian influence in the region. And so Egypt began flexing its muscles, strengthening its own military presence in the area. Judah was thus caught in the middle of a power struggle between what we might now call superpowers. Judah became subject to Egypt for a time, but after the defeat of the Egyptians at Carchemish in 605 BCE, Judah became subject to Babylon.

The conflict in the region rumbled on, and after a partial Egyptian victory over Babylon in 601 BCE, King Jehoiakim of Judah saw the chance to strike a blow and revolted against the weakened Babylon. A fierce siege of Jerusalem followed at the end of 598 BCE and finally, in 597 BCE, Jerusalem fell to the Babylonians. King

Nebuchadnezzar of Babylon wreaked a fierce revenge on Jerusalem for its rebelliousness. He looted and pillaged the city mercilessly.

Significantly, this destruction included the looting of the Temple. He carried off the treasures of the Temple and of the royal palace. What he didn't take with him he destroyed. He bore off not just precious metals and jewels, but people as well. 'He carried all Jerusalem off into exile, all the nobles and all the notables, ten thousand of these were exiled, with all the blacksmiths and metalworkers; only the poorest people in the country were left behind.' (2 Kgs 24:13-14) Being one of the 'notables' mentioned in the account in the Second Book of Kings – he was a priest – Ezekiel was among those who were carried off to Babylon.

According to what he says at the start of the book, Ezekiel began prophesying to the people in the fifth year of the exile, 593 BCE. The first two-thirds of the book are made up of oracles where the prophet explains to the exiled Israelites just how unfaithful they had been and just how much wrath and punishment they had earned; as well as oracles against some foreign powers and foes. A lot of this material is quite a challenge to read, and some of it borders on the obscene, employing language around conjugal infidelity that sounds coarse to modern ears. The reading we hear at the Easter Vigil comes from the final section of the book, which presents visions of restoration and healing for Israel and for a new temple.

Judah's exile in Babylon was the historical and political context for Ezekiel's words, but the religious and spiritual context is more important. We should not underestimate the extent of the trauma inherent in the exile. It was not migration. It was not merely geographic dislocation. It was the complete destruction of their self-understanding. The people of Israel had understood themselves to be God's chosen people, blessed by their covenant with him; they believed that they had been given the Land by the

Seventh Reading • Ezekiel 36:16-28

Lord God; that David's line would reign in Jerusalem; and that God would dwell among them in the Temple. The exile was an earthquake, shattering that lofty edifice. They lost the land, the royal city, the Temple and the monarchy. With this trauma would have come the inevitable questioning of whether they could still claim to be God's Chosen People. The sense of dislocation is expressed well in the familiar words of Psalm 137: 'By the rivers of Babylon there we sat and wept, remembering Zion.... O how would we sing the song of the Lord on alien soil?' (Ps 137:1, 4)

Much of the book of Ezekiel would have been of cold comfort to the disorientated Israelites. The prophet repeatedly points out to the exiled Israelites the numerous ways in which they had broken their covenant with the Almighty, drawn God's wrath upon them, and suffered well-deserved and terrible punishment. Yes, they had a covenant with the Almighty, but they had proved false to it. They worshipped idols, even allowing idols in the Temple, and had not obeyed the moral law. Yes, they had been granted the Land, but they had forfeited their right to it by their infidelities. Yes, the Lord God had made promises to King David and his descendants, but they had ruled unjustly and mistreated their people. Yes, the Lord had promised to dwell in the Temple, but they had so polluted the place with their blasphemies that God was abandoning it, and without his protective presence the city would fall.

Divine Initiative

This was the context into which Ezekiel spoke the words in the passage we hear proclaimed at the Easter Vigil. We can divide the passage into two sections. The first is addressed to Ezekiel only. It is like the background briefing note, written by an adviser, that a modern politician might be given along with the text of the speech he or she has to deliver. The core message is simple: God's people have sinned. They worshipped idols. Their behaviour disgusted God and he unleashed his fury and scattered them from their homeland. This is significant. He is saying that the exile wasn't just the result of Nebuchadnezzar's victory; it was God's punishment. And they deserved it. 'I sentenced them as their conduct and actions deserved'. (36:19)

Nevertheless, deserved or not, their exile was causing scandal. The very fact of God's own people being thrown out of their homeland by the Lord God didn't reflect well on anyone, including the Almighty himself. People were saying, 'these are the people of the Lord; [and yet] they have been exiled from his land'. (36:20) To use the language of the business world, their continuing exile constituted a reputational risk to the Almighty and he wanted to address it. 'I have been concerned about my holy name, which the House of Israel has profaned among the nations where they have gone'. (36:21) Other nations might interpret the continuing exile of the Israelites from the Promised Land as a sign that the Lord God had been either unwilling – or, worse, unable – to protect his people from the depredations of Nebuchadnezzar.

And so God decides to take action. He has a message for Ezekiel to announce to the Israelites. That message is the second part of the Easter Vigil reading. In summary: God is going to intervene. He is going to get involved, not to punish them further, but to restore them. It is striking that he is doing so not because his heart is softening regarding their sinfulness, but because he wants to vindicate his own name. He will not restore them 'for your sake, House of Israel, but for the sake of my holy name, which has been profaned among the nations, where you have gone'. (36:22)

The voice of the Lord God refers to his name four times in this passage. We know from the encounter between Moses and the Lord at the burning bush that God's name is sacred above and beyond all other things. The divine Name was so sacred that it could not

Seventh Reading • Ezekiel 36:16-28

be uttered and is still not pronounced aloud by devout Jews. The exile was an affront to the sublime holiness of God's name and he announces through Ezekiel that he is going to vindicate it. What he is promising is a manifestation of his sovereign power, whereby he will show Israel and the nations among whom they had been scattered, that he is indeed the Holy and Almighty One. Just in case anyone might be left in doubt...

There is something very striking here and it causes some Scripture scholars and not a few preachers some serious consternation. If we read the text carefully, we see that God is not actually demanding repentance from his wayward people. Neither is he threatening further disaster if they don't abandon their sinful ways. *He* himself is taking the initiative. He is acting freely so as to show his holiness and the power of his name at work among his people. 'And the nations will learn that I am the Lord ... when I display my holiness for your sake before their eyes'. (36:23)

What he promises truly is restoration and renewal. Whereas in the first section the people were scattered, he now promises that he will gather them and bring them home. This will be a new Exodus. Whereas in the first section he describes them as unclean and defiled by blood, in the promise of restoration he pledges to purify them: 'I shall pour clean water over you and you will be cleansed; I shall cleanse you of all your idols'. (36:25) Note the references to clean water and cleansing. It is no surprise that this text has been added to the Easter liturgy to underscore the baptismal theme of the Vigil.

But the promise of divine intervention does not end there. When God intervenes there is always more. Not only is God going to reverse the effects of his people's sinful ways, he is going to give them the means of remaining faithful to the covenant in future. Not only is he going to gather them and bring them back and wash away their guilt, he is going to give them his spirit – a spirit that will transform them. 'I shall give you a *new* heart, and put a *new* spirit in you'. (36:26) He is not just going to turn back the clock, but rather he is going to do something *new*. Their hard and stubborn hearts will be replaced with hearts of flesh and infused with God's own breath. This spirit will equip them for fidelity, so that they will keep God's laws and respect his commandments. (36:27) God's action here is his alone. It is not a response to their conversion. As one scholar has written: 'This is no turn of heart on the Israelites' part but a heart transplant performed unilaterally by [the Lord God] to ensure the people's utter and unending obedience.'[2]

The outcome of this divine intervention is to be a renewed covenant: 'You shall be my people and I shall be your God'. (36:28) The image of God taking away their heart of stone and giving them a heart of flesh is particularly striking and evocative. The transformation of the heart from stone to flesh is a transformation that alters a mind-set of death to one of life and love. Equally powerful, yet easily overlooked, is the promise that God will put his spirit in them. He says it twice. He says that he will 'put a new spirit' in them, and later reinforces it with 'I shall put my spirit in you, and make you keep my laws, and sincerely respect my observances'. (36:27) Maybe that is the truly new thing that he is going to do – breathing his own breath on them and in them, so that they will be equipped to walk in his ways, and so keep the covenant that he is making with them, defining afresh the relationship whereby they will be his people and he will be their God.

Clean Water

The pouring of water and the giving of God's spirit also clearly evoke the sacraments of Christian initiation, and in particular,

[2]. Katheryn Pfisterer Darr, 'The Book of Ezekiel', *The New Interpreter's Bible*, Vol. VI (Nashville: Abingdon Press, 2001), 1492.

Seventh Reading • Ezekiel 36:16-28

Baptism. The initiation of new Christians by Baptism, Confirmation and admission to the Eucharist formed part of the liturgy of Easter night from earliest times. Already in the second century Tertullian wrote: 'The Passover provides the day of most solemnity for Baptism, for then was accomplished our Lord's Passion, and into it we are baptised.'[3] Somehow, this fell out of common practice. Vestiges remained though, with the blessing of the 'Easter water', at the Easter Vigil, which in the Tridentine rite took place on Holy Saturday morning.

When the rites were revised and restored by Pope Pius XII in 1951, the renewal of baptismal promises was added. This was certainly an enrichment. It underscored the link – obvious, but not always appreciated – between the water that was being blessed at the Vigil and the baptismal covenant of the faithful who were present.

The revised rites as we received them in the 1970s restored the actual celebration of the sacraments of initiation to the Vigil. Though this was nothing more than the restoration of the practice of the early Church, it was revolutionary and completely transformed the way many people experience the Easter Vigil. It is the most appropriate time to celebrate the three sacraments of initiation. Christian Initiation at the Vigil is at its most powerful when *adults* are baptised, confirmed and nourished with the Bread of Life and the Cup of Salvation for the first time, during it.

The liturgy as we have it now almost presumes that there will be Baptisms during the Easter Vigil and it is presumably for that reason that the reading from Ezekiel was added in the post-conciliar reforms. Each of the Old Testament readings at the Easter Vigil is followed by a responsorial psalm and in one or two cases there are two options. The reading from Ezekiel is one of them. Psalm 42 is always an option, with the response, 'Like the deer that yearns

---

3. Tertullian, *De Baptismo*, 19.

for running streams, so my soul is yearning for you my God'. It is clearly a suitable complement to the reading, with its themes of thirsting to enter the Temple and see God, trusting in God to guide us, thanksgiving to God and asking for God's light and truth. The image of a deer was a common motif in the decoration of early Christian baptisteries. Deer were often depicted with serpents in their mouths, on account of the belief that they could eat snakes and suffer no harm. For those preparing for Baptism, the implications were that they would, like the deer, be able to drink of the 'running streams' of paradise, experienced in Baptism, only after they had devoured the serpents of evil.[4]

> The flesh is washed that the soul may be made spotless: the flesh is anointed that the soul may be consecrated: the flesh is signed [with the cross] that the soul too may be protected: the flesh is overshadowed by the imposition of the hand that the soul also may be illumined by the Spirit: the flesh feeds on the Body and Blood of Christ so that the soul as well may be filled with God
>
> TERTULLIAN
> *De resurrectione carnis*

Psalm 42 is an option whether there are to be Baptisms or not. However, if Baptism is to be celebrated, there is an option for a different psalm – Psalm 51, with the response, 'A pure heart create for me, O God'. This is an interesting possibility. Psalm 51 is the famous *Miserere* psalm, the most important of the penitential psalms. Various parts of this psalm weave in and out of the liturgy throughout the season of Lent, and it forms part of the Liturgy of the Hours on every Friday throughout the year. It is almost counter-intuitive to sing such a sombre penitential song right in the middle of the Easter Vigil, just before the joyful moment when the *Gloria* is sung, the bells are rung and the altar candles are lit.

---

4. See Jean Daniélou, *The Bible and the Liturgy* (Notre Dame: University of Notre Dame Press, 1966), 36, 97.

Seventh Reading • Ezekiel 36:16-28

The reason for Psalm 51's inclusion is that it contains much of the same language as the promise made by the Lord God in Ezekiel's prophecy. In the reading God promised a new heart and a new spirit, while the psalmist asks: 'A pure heart create for me, O God, put a steadfast spirit within me.' In the reading God promised that his spirit would make Israel keep his laws and respect his commands, while the psalmist asks: 'Give me again the joy of your help; with a spirit of fervour sustain me.' Somewhat bizarrely, the compilers of the lectionary chose to omit verse 4 of the psalm, even though it might seem the most appropriate verse in the whole psalm for this baptismal context: 'O wash me more and more from my guilt and cleanse me from my sin.'

Aside from the inclusion of Gospel readings from Mark and Luke, allowing for a different Gospel passage for each year of the three-year lectionary cycle, there are two readings in the modern Easter Vigil that were introduced for the first time in 1970. As noted above, the reading from Ezekiel is one. The reading from the Letter to the Romans is the other. The latter has an even stronger and more explicit baptismal focus and in a real sense prompts us to listen to the joyful Gospel proclamation that follows it through the lens of our having been made sharers in Christ's Resurrection through Baptism.

Ezekiel announced God's unilateral renewal of the covenant with his people with cleansing water and the giving of a new spirit. In his rising from the tomb Christ Jesus unsealed the fountain from which God's people may draw this cleansing water, receive the anointing of his Spirit and experience *new* life. 'You are not baptised in ordinary water, but in the water of second birth. Now ordinary water cannot become this other thing except by the coming of the Holy Spirit.'[5]

Ezekiel's words are a reminder that the long series of Old Testa-

---

5. Theodore of Mopsuestia, *Baptismal Homily 3*.

ment readings which it brings to an end are not just edifying stories and are not just about the past. They invite us to realise that we are involved and that we share in Christ's Paschal Mystery. They are a powerful reminder that God is always present and active in his creation, that the life flowing from the Resurrection of Christ Jesus is freely given to us in Baptism, and that the transforming power of his Holy Spirit is his abiding gift. As St Cyril of Jerusalem taught the newly-baptised in Jerusalem in the fourth century, we too are anointed ones:

> It is right to call you 'Christs' or anointed ones.... When you emerged from the pool of sacred waters you were anointed in a manner corresponding with Christ's anointing. That anointing is the Holy Spirit.... Now that you are reckoned worthy of this holy anointing, you are called Christians, and this title you substantiate by your new birth.[6]

Questions for Reflection or Discussion

What light does this reading shed for you on the Paschal Mystery of Christ's Passion, Death and Resurrection?

What would it mean for you to receive a 'new heart' and a 'new spirit' and how might you thus reflect the glory of Christ's resurrection to those around you?

---

6. Cyril of Jerusalem, *Mystagogical Catechesis 3*.

8

Baptised into Christ Jesus – Alive for God
Eighth Reading • Romans 6:3-11

MARY T. O'BRIEN, P.B.V.M.

Introduction

In the pre-Vatican II Holy Week Office of *Tenebrae* (the word itself means 'shadows'), long Scripture readings were read in Latin while the church candles were slowly quenched, one by one, until the congregation was left in total darkness and silence. Even though, as a child, I did not understand a word that was spoken, I was carried emotionally into the darkness and emptiness of that space beyond words, in the long shadow of the Cross. When the lights went on afterwards as we left the church, we tasted the joy of being able to see again, of being once more in the light. That ceremony of *Tenebrae* left a lasting impression on me. It still speaks something of the essence of Holy Saturday as an in-between time, between darkness and light, between death and life.

Holy Saturday is still meant to be, liturgically, a place in the shadows, in the space between darkness and light. Holy Saturday reaches into the depths and heights of human experience. Whereas in our liturgical calendar, Holy Saturday comes around once a year, for one day only, that is not always so in life. Any of us who has suffered the loss of a loved one will know that one does not move from Good Friday to Easter Sunday in just one day. For some people Holy Saturday can last months, years, even a lifetime. Holy Saturday is iconic, reflective of the highs and lows on life's journey. The liturgical celebration of the Easter Vigil, in the night between Holy Saturday and Easter Sunday, encompasses the depths and heights of human experience, taking humanity with Christ to the sepulchre and the depths of Sheol, only to raise it up with Christ in Resurrection victory. The excerpt from Paul's Letter to the Romans which is proclaimed as the Eighth Reading in the Vigil, and the first from the New Testament, respects the 'in-between' nature of the time and lifts it to another plane.

Baptised in His Death

The proclamation of the passage from Romans scales the depths and heights of what it means to be a disciple of Jesus Christ, but it is by no means an easy read. It has been the subject of much scholarly discussion over the years. The first sentence may be considered as a kind of summary of the entire passage:

> When we were baptised in Christ Jesus we were baptised in his death; in other words when we were baptised we went into the tomb with him and joined him in death, so that, as Christ was raised from the dead by the Father's glory, we too might live a new life. (Rom 6:3-4)

There is quite a lot of action and movement in that sentence. According to St Paul, we have been baptised *into* Christ Jesus, baptised *into* his death. We even went *into* the tomb with him, *joining* him in death. The first reaction in response to such extraordinary statements might be to question how this could be so. Most of us cannot remember our own Baptism. But we may have had the experience of being present at the Baptism of someone else. Do you think of your Baptism, or any Baptism, as a death? What are we to make of these words from St Paul? It is obvious that we are not meant to understand them literally. We know that we have not physically gone into the tomb with Jesus. So, what could the phrase 'baptised in Christ Jesus' possibly mean?

As always, when we come across a challenging text in the Bible, we set about interpreting it. One approach is to seek to extract meaning from the text by breaking it up, analysing every word, studying the sentence structure, grammar and syntax, before reassembling the parts again in the hope that the text will yield a meaning, or perhaps several meanings.

Another approach is to look at the text as a whole, to treat it as if it were a work of art in three dimensions. We can then, as it were, walk all around it and survey it from different angles, examining the context in which it is set, how it belongs within that context and what it contributes to that context. In that scenario the diverse viewpoints open to possible understandings.

In this chapter we will employ this second method, looking at the reading: (a) in the context of the Easter Vigil liturgy; (b) in the context of Paul's Letter to the Romans; and (c) in the context of other relevant New Testament writings

The Easter Vigil

The celebration of the Easter Vigil, or the 'Mother of all Vigils', as St Augustine described it, begins after dark on Holy Saturday night. The celebration usually begins outdoors in darkness with a service of light, or *lucernarium*. This is followed by a longer than usual Liturgy of the Word, with seven readings from the Old Testament and two from the New Testament, including the extract from the Letter to the Romans under consideration here, each accompanied by a psalm and a prayer. After the seventh and final reading from the Old Testament, with its accompanying psalm and prayer, there comes an interlude – a breathing space – where the altar candles are lit, the *Gloria* is sung, and the church bells are rung. This is followed by the Collect, with promises of illumination and renewal. We pray: 'O God, who make this most sacred night radiant with the glory of the Lord's Resurrection, stir up in your Church a spirit of adoption, so that, renewed in body and mind, we may render you undivided service'.

The reading from Paul's Letter to the Romans comes at a crucial moment, a turning point in the liturgy. It anticipates the Baptismal Liturgy that follows the Gospel and homily. At this 'in-between' juncture, it serves a kind of bridging role. It is still part of the Liturgy of the Word, but it points us towards the Baptismal Liturgy. Members of the congregation will have words from the Collect, such as 'radiant', 'stir up' and 'renewed', still ringing in their ears. Or they may well recall Ezekiel's words already proclaimed, carrying God's promise of the gift of a new heart and spirit.

There are hints of newness in the air. It is rising time, a time for awakening from sleep, for moving out of the darkness. Here, as the focus turns to the baptismal font and those to be baptised (or to the renewal of baptismal vows), all are invited to undertake that baptismal journey from darkness to light, from death to life.

The Letter to the Romans

Paul's Letter to the Romans, made up of 16 chapters, is his longest letter, and is generally regarded as the most important. Apart from its length, it is a challenging read because of the complexity of some of its arguments and because Paul employs a type of argumentation and persuasion that is quite unfamiliar to us today. But this wonderful letter is foundational in many ways for a large part of Christian theology. It expresses a lot of what Christian faith thinks about God and what God has done in Christ. Like all of Paul's writings, it is heavily laced with references and allusions to the Hebrew Scriptures.

In chapter 5, the chapter before the one from which our reading comes, Paul engages in a dramatic portrayal of Adam and Christ – Adam, as head of unredeemed humanity, and Christ, as

Eighth Reading • Romans 6:3-11

head of redeemed humanity. The unredeemed human race, a great body under the dominion of sin, is identified with and incorporated into Adam. The members constitute one body with Adam, incorporated into him, as head, while the redeemed human race, under the dominion of grace, is identified with and incorporated into Christ as Head.

Paul compares the two realms – the realm of sin and the realm of grace – and argues that grace will triumph, no matter how powerful the realm of sin. Grace outweighs sin in Paul's view, because 'however great the number of sins committed, grace was even greater'. (5:20) Paul's enemies had read this as a licence to sin more and more, so that grace would triumph more and more. But to claim that would be a misreading of the Gospel and of Paul's teaching.

And so, chapter 6 begins with Paul asking the question: 'Does it follow that we should remain in sin so as to let grace have greater scope?' (6:1-2). The answer comes with a strong *'mê genoito'* ('no, no way!') followed by the passage which is proclaimed at the Easter Vigil. This passage, when read in context, is not primarily a teaching about Baptism. But Paul invokes Baptism as part of his argument against those who accuse him of false teaching. It is Paul's attempt at answering the accusation that people should go on sinning because the more they sin the more grace will abound. He defends his teaching by reminding his readers of the meaning of their Baptism. It is a dying to sin. It is costly and utterly demanding. It involves a definitive break with a sinful way of life. It means becoming one with Christ Jesus, incorporated into his Body, becoming one with him in a death like his, going the whole way with him, being identified with him.

Paul reminds his readers that this has been signified already by their going down into the baptismal pool, being immersed and drenched in its waters, emerging as new people, dressed in new clothes, set on a new path – the path of new life, life in Christ. Being 'baptised into Christ' has ethical and moral implications.

It is not grace on the cheap. Being 'baptised into the death of Christ' involves death to the dominion of sin. This means entering a new realm of allegiance – the realm of grace. It is important to note that this interpretation of Baptism, though not the only one found in Paul's writings, is one of the oldest. According to Thomas H. Tobin, 'Paul's interpretation of Baptism as a Baptism into Christ's death marks the first appearance of this interpretation in early Christianity.'[1]

The idea of being 'co-buried' with Christ (*sunthaptô*) is interesting. The Greek word used is rare in Paul's vocabulary. The word 'with' indicates a mutual relationship with Christ, a relationship so close that it merges into identification with him: what applies to Christ applies to the baptised. In Baptism, God buried us along with Jesus Christ. This obviously does not mean that God put us into the same tomb as Jesus and laid us down beside him. But Paul's message is unambiguous. Baptism is a radical turning away from the power of sin. It is a radical turning towards Christ and identification with him.

> In the grave of the water the priest buries the whole man; and he resuscitates him by the power of life that is hidden in his words.... With a mystery of our Redeemer the one that is baptised goes into the bosom of the font after the manner of those three days in the midst of the tomb. Three days was our Redeemer with the dead: so also he that is baptised – the three times are three days. He truly dies by a symbol of that death which the Enlivener of all died; and he surely lives with a type of the life without end. Sin and death he puts off and casts away in baptism, after the manner of those garments which our Lord departing left in the tomb.
>
> NARSAI, Homily 21

---

1. Thomas H. Tobin, *Paul's Rhetoric in its Contexts* (Peabody, MA: Hendrickson, 2004), 198.

Eighth Reading • Romans 6:3-11

Other New Testament Interpretations of Baptism

A look at the word 'baptism' and the verb 'baptise' may help us further. When St Paul was writing, that particular verb could denote quite a few things. It could signify immersion in water or being plunged or drenched in water. It could, more rarely, signify washing or cleansing or even sprinkling.[2] However, in trying to grasp something of the depth of what Paul is talking about in this reading, we need to look elsewhere in the New Testament for other uses of the terms 'baptism', 'to be baptised' and, more especially, 'baptised into'. There are many types of baptism in the New Testament, and most of these do not involve water. Examples include Baptism for the forgiveness of sins (Matt 3:6; Acts 2:38), baptism in the Holy Spirit (Luke 3:16; 1 Cor 12:13), baptism into suffering (Luke 12:50; Mark 10:38), baptism into Moses (1 Cor 10:2), and baptism in water (Matt 3:16; Mark1:5, 9-10; Acts 8:36).

When Jesus says, in Luke's Gospel (Luke 12:50), 'there is a baptism I must still receive, and how great is my distress till it is over', he cannot be talking about his own baptism in the Jordan, because that has already happened. He is obviously talking about some suffering or ordeal that he is to undergo in the future. And when he says to his close followers, James and John, the sons of Zebedee, with their high notions about sitting on his right and left in the Kingdom: 'Can you drink the cup that I must drink, or be baptised with the baptism with which I must be baptised?' (Mark 10:38) he is talking about something ominous, something that is likely to prove too much for the two brothers. In both instances, Jesus is referring to his forthcoming Passion and death as his baptism. This is important for an understanding of our reading.

---

2. Joseph A. Fitzmyer, 'Romans,' *NJBC* (Upper Saddle River, NJ: Prentice Hall, 1990), 847.

Other Pauline Interpretations of Baptism

Noting that there are many understandings of Baptism in the Gospels, and that Paul in his Letter to the Romans describes Baptism as a death, as entry into the tomb with Jesus, it will be helpful to consider just three or four examples from other Pauline letters, which throw light on what Paul says in his Letter to the Christians in Rome.

In his First Letter to the Corinthians (1 Cor 10:1-4), Paul speaks of the Hebrews being guided by a cloud above them and passing through the sea. He says that they were 'baptised into Moses'. This is clearly a reference to the Exodus experience, where the Hebrews, led by Moses, were rescued from slavery in Egypt and moulded into a covenant people, with Moses as their head and representative before God.

The account of this event is proclaimed as the Third Reading of the Easter Vigil. In Israel's sacred story, the Exodus journey marks the creation of a new people, a covenant people, henceforth 'shackled' or bound in chains of love to the God who saves. All of God's dealings with Israel from that moment onwards are portrayed as accomplished through Moses. The Lord God and Israel have become one body. 'Baptised into Moses', this liberated people becomes a corporate body with Moses as head.

Does Paul have the Exodus event in mind when writing to Rome? All indications are that he does, even though he does not say so. He sees Christians who have been baptised into Christ Jesus as incorporated into a new Body, with Christ as its Head, the new People of God. Just as Israel was 'baptised into Moses', incorporated into one body with Moses as head, now God's new people are 'baptised into Christ Jesus', one with the entire body of believers under Christ as Head.

This is confirmed by what he says later to the Corinthians (1 Cor 12:13): 'In the one Spirit we were all baptised, Jews as well as Greeks, slaves as well as citizens, and one Spirit was given to us all to drink.'

If one considers Paul's interpretation of Baptism in the third chapter of the letter to the Galatians, another perspective opens. Addressing Christian believers in Galatia, he reminds them that they are children of God through faith: 'All baptised in Christ, you have all clothed yourselves in Christ, and there are no more distinctions between Jew and Greek, slave and free, male and female, but all of you are one in Christ Jesus.' (Gal 3:27-28) This is a difficult passage and it raises many questions which do not concern us here.[3]

> I am your forgiveness, I am the Passover of your salvation, I am the Lamb which was sacrificed for you, I am your ransom, I am your light, I am your saviour, I am your resurrection, I am your king, I am leading you up to the heights of heaven, I will show you the eternal Father, I will raise you up by my right hand.
>
> MELITO OF SARDIS, *Peri Pascha*

However, it does help us to understand something more of what Paul is saying in the passage from Romans that we hear at the Easter Vigil. When he speaks of being 'baptised in Christ', in addressing the Galatians, he speaks of a metaphorical 'clothing in Christ', most probably informed by experience of newly-baptised persons emerging from the baptismal pool to be dressed in new clothes as a sign of the new life they have embraced. In reminding his Galatian audience of their Baptism, Paul calls on them to avoid all divisions, reminding them that in Baptism they were all 'clothed in Christ'. Elsewhere in the Letter to the Romans (13:11-14), Paul also speaks of putting on Christ, although in that context he speaks more in terms of putting on the armour of Christ, so as to be ready for battle against sin, rather than donning normal garments.

3. Tobin, *Paul's Rhetoric*, 199.

The Letter to the Colossians speaks of growth in Christian faith as enabling the believer to live a better life, 'so you will be able to lead the kind of life the Lord expects of you, a life acceptable to him in all its aspects'. (Col 1:10) This is seen as thanks to the inner strength provided by the Father's power. 'Because that is what he has done: he has taken us out of the power of darkness and created a place for us in the kingdom of the Son that he loves; and in him we gain our freedom, the forgiveness of our sins.' (Col 1:14) This text, in its interpretation of baptismal initiation as a transfer from one realm to another, from the realm of darkness to the realm of light, is close to the interpretation given in the Romans text that we hear at the Easter Vigil. Both underline the ethical implications of this transfer. Transfer to life 'in him' (in Christ) means 'freedom and the forgiveness of our sins'.

Conclusion

These sample texts on Baptism, while illuminative one of another and helpful in understanding the text of Romans 6:3-11, do not, individually or in total, provide a complete sacramental theology of Baptism. The Church's sacramental theology of Baptism evolved over several centuries, incorporating for example, the understanding of Baptism found in John's Gospel, which focuses on the ideas of re-birth or new birth.

But we have some important foundational elements here in the samples taken from the Pauline corpus – dying and rising with Christ, being incorporated into the body of Christ, being clothed with Christ, being transferred from one realm (the realm of darkness) to another realm (the realm of light). Vorgrimler summarises it well: 'Rom 6:1-11 is a comprehensive exposition of the reasons for the new ethical life of Christians; it is not a sacramental-theological explanation of Baptism.'[4]

Raymond Brown reminds us that Paul's treatment of Baptism in Romans 6:3-11 is the longest treatment of that topic in the Pauline letters, and he suggests that Paul may be re-using one of his baptismal sermons here in his Letter to the Romans.[5] Be that as it may, we also note that the text we are considering is rich with echoes of the Hebrew Bible, especially the Exodus narrative. It offers a vision of Baptism as a veritable sharing in the New Exodus – that of Christ in his death and Resurrection. This is presented as part of Paul's argument about the two realms – the realm of sin and the realm of grace, which equate with the realm of Adam and the realm of Christ. Anyone in the realm of Christ is dead to sin, freed from the dominion of sin. Anyone 'baptised in Christ Jesus' is 'alive to God' – alive because now sharing in the life of the Risen Lord.

Questions for Reflection or Discussion

Re-read the passage, replacing the pronouns 'we' and 'our' with 'I' and 'my'. What do you understand by the idea that you were baptised into Christ's death and went into the tomb with him?

The reading says that we too must be 'dead to sin but alive for God in Christ Jesus'. How can that idea translate into your daily living?

---

4. Herbert Vorgrimler. *Sacramental Theology* (Collegeville MN: Liturgical Press, 1992, 104.
5. Raymond E. Brown. *Introduction to the New Testament* (New York: Doubleday, 1989), 568.

9

Dawning

Gospel, Year A • Matthew 28:1-10

CÉLINE MANGAN, O.P.

'Dawning' could be the theme of Matthew's Resurrection story. It begins with the words, 'after the Sabbath', where the word translated as 'after' has the connotation of 'late' – so late in fact that it becomes 'after'. This is what the next phrase implies: 'towards dawn on the first day of the week', or, as one commentator puts it, 'as the Sabbath *faded* into the dawn of the first day'.[1] We are in that magical time of the day, just before sunrise, when the promise of all that is to come is before us, as it was for the women who came to the tomb. The story goes on to tell of their dawning understanding of what had happened. They thought they were coming to visit a grave to mourn the death of their loved one.[2] Instead, it gradually dawned on them that something altogether unexpected had taken place.

The angel they encounter at the tomb invites them to 'Come and see', but what they actually see is an emptiness: 'the *place* where he lay'. (Matt 28:6) The body of Jesus was no longer there. A new light had dawned on the world, just as it had at the begin-

---

1. Michael Mullins, *The Gospel of Matthew* (Dublin: Columba Press, 2007), 613.
2. *Semahot* 8:1; see Daniel J. Harrington, *The Gospel of Matthew*, SP1 (Collegeville, MN: Liturgical Press, 1991), 409. Matthew does not have the women come to anoint, as Jesus had already been anointed for burial (26: 6-13).

ning of creation when God said 'Let there be light'. (Gen 1:3). What are the women to make of it all?

Drama

Matthew answers that question in a very dramatic way. First of all, he tells of the occurrence of a violent earthquake (the word is *seismos*, from which we get our term 'seismic'); then an angel of extraordinary appearance is to be seen. (28:2-3) This is apocalyptic language, used already by Matthew in Jesus' discourse about the end times in chapter 24. The purpose of this apocalyptic language was to usher in the coming of God's kingdom, 'and this good news of the kingdom will be proclaimed throughout the world.' (24:14)

There is a very strong link between Matthew's Resurrection account and that of the Transfiguration. Just as there it was said of Jesus that 'his face shone like the sun and his clothes became as white as the light', (17:2) so now the angel's 'face was like lightning, his robe white as snow'. As Jesus, on the Mount of Transfiguration, made the link for his disciples between his suffering and Resurrection, so now the angel tells the women: 'I know you are looking for Jesus, who was crucified. He is not here.' (28:5-6). Just as the Transfiguration account has the voice of the Father telling the disciples that they are to listen to the words of Jesus, so now the women quickly move from the angel's words to those of Jesus himself.

The function of angels in Matthew's Gospel was to communicate God's message and to interpret it. In the stories around the birth of Jesus it was an angel who communicated to Joseph what would happen and who interpreted those happenings for him: the one to be born will be Emmanuel, 'God is with us' (1:23). So here at the tomb the angel interprets the emptiness for the women and communicates to them the great act of God in raising Jesus from the dead. Matthew's Gospel is highly structured with its end coming full circle to its beginning: the Gospel starts with *birth* and ends with *rebirth*. Just as at the *birth* God's presence is proclaimed in the name 'Emmanuel', so now at the *rebirth* there is a new manifestation of God's presence to God's people.

It is obvious that the Resurrection had already happened before the angel rolled back the stone. I love the very human touch Matthew gives by saying 'he sat upon it'. (28:2) I remember a musician who did some wonderful antiphons for the Easter liturgy and her music for that phrase was like someone plonking down!

The Guards

Matthew's is the only Gospel to mention the guards at the tomb, following on from the end of his Passion narrative, where the chief priests and the Pharisees come to Pilate to demand that the tomb be made secure in case the disciples would steal the body (27:62-66). The passage after our one (28:11-15) will have the guards telling the chief priests what they had seen and being told to say that it was while they were asleep that the disciples came and stole the body.

But our text is at pains to point out that they were anything but asleep: they were in so much fear from the dramatic occurrences that 'they were like dead men'. (28:4) There is irony in the text between the guards, who are supposedly very much alive but are 'like dead men', and Jesus, who was dead but is now very much alive. There is also a great contrast between the guards who suffered a numbing fear, and the women who are relieved of their fear when the angel speaks to them: 'You', the angel said, 'have nothing to fear'. (28:5 NEB)

Like all those who come to Jesus throughout the Gospel, the women can confidently expect to encounter the Presence of God in Jesus, the Risen Lord. Judaism spoke of the Presence of God as the *Shekhina* and they imaged the *Shekhina* as being with them, especially in times of trouble. For example, in one Jewish writing, it is said: 'Wherever Israel went into exile, the Shekhina, as it were, was exiled with them; they were exiled to Egypt, the Shekhina was with them ... they were exiled to Babylon, the Shekhina was with them.'[3] Jesus, through his Passion and Resurrection, has become that Presence of God for Christians.

Resurrection

A recent book on the Resurrection is entitled, *Is This All There Is?*[4] This is the question which all the Resurrection accounts attempt to answer and which Matthew's Gospel does in a unique way. What all the Resurrection stories emphasise is that whatever happened after the death of Jesus changed a frightened group of followers into ardent promoters and preachers of the fact that Jesus had risen. They believed that Jesus was living among them.

Belief in Resurrection was a slow development among the people of Israel. In fact there are only a few late texts where God's overcoming of death is clearly portrayed, the clearest being that of Daniel 12:2: 'And many of those who sleep in the dust shall awake, some to everlasting life, and some to shame and everlasting contempt.'[5] One of the great themes of the Hebrew Scriptures was that of deliverance, deliverance from Egypt in the Exodus in the first instance, as the Third Reading of the Vigil so eloquently reminds us. But that experience of deliverance was continued throughout their history and can be seen as a backdrop to their gradual realisation of an eternal deliverance.[6] So that, even if there

---

3. *Mekhilta de-R. Ismael* (Massekhta de-Pisha, xiv, 51-52) as quoted in Ephraim E. Urbach, *The Sages* (Cambridge: Harvard University Press, 1975), 43.
4. Gerhard Lohfink, *Is This All There Is? On Resurrection and Eternal Life*, trans. L. M. Maloney (Collegeville, MN: Liturgical Press, 2018).
5. See Harrington, *The Gospel of Matthew*, 411-412.
6. See the Jewish writer Jon D. Levenson, *Resurrection and the Restoration of*

was not explicit belief in resurrection in earlier parts of the Bible, there is clearly an intimation, especially in some psalms, that the person who has been held by God's right hand cannot sink back into nothingness. For example, Psalm 16 says: 'You show me the path of life. In your presence there is fullness of joy: in your right hand are pleasures forevermore.' (Ps 16:11). Of course when the psalm was written it referred to pleasures in this life, but as it was recited down the ages it came to open up to future possibilities. Today, it is a psalm that is very helpful to pray with people who are dying.

> The resurrection of Christ responds to the intuitions, to the hopes of a human destiny open to the future, and addresses our desire that death does not have the last word in life, that the placing of the stone at the tomb is not the last act of our existence.
>
> CARLO MARIA MARTINI
> *I Believe in Eternal Life*

There were other possible ways for the early Church to think of life after death, besides resurrection. Like the Greeks they could have spoken of the immortality of the soul which would leave the body behind. But the Jewish world considered body and soul as one entity: an enfleshed soul, or an animated body. At the same time, they realised that the body as we know it decays. So, Paul, for example, would say, 'what is sown is perishable, what is raised is imperishable' (1 Cor 15:42). There is the realisation that even though the body as we know it dies, the whole person's lived life is caught up into God. Judaism in Jesus' time believed that this would occur at the end of time.

The great insight of the early Church was that this had already happened with the Resurrection of Jesus and would happen for

---

Israel (New Haven: Yale University Press, 2006): 'When the belief in resurrection finally makes an unambiguous appearance in Judaism, it is thus both an innovation and a restatement of a tension that had pervaded the religion of Israel from the beginning, a tension between the Lord's promise of life, on the one hand, and the reality of death, on the other' (216).

all of us at death. As the Epistle of the Vigil puts it so succinctly: 'But we believe that having died with Christ we shall return to life with him.' (Rom 6:8). The dawning realisation of the women in Matthew's story mirrors the wonder of the early Christians' understanding of what the Resurrection of Jesus meant for them and for us.[7]

The Women

All the Gospels speak of the women witnesses to the Passion and Resurrection of Jesus, a fact that must have been deeply embedded in the tradition. The names of the women vary, Mary of Magdala being the only constant. From her role in witnessing to the Resurrection she is rightly considered today as the 'Apostle to the Apostles',[8] rather than as the 'sinful woman' of past centuries. In fact, nowhere in the Gospels is Mary of Magdala spoken of as a prostitute. Calling her *Apostola Apostolorum* goes back to Rabanus Maurus, a Benedictine monk of the ninth century.[9] The phrase was happily taken up by St Thomas Aquinas. Indeed Mary Magdalene is considered a Patroness of the Order of Preachers because of her role as preacher.[10] Her liturgy in the Dominican Calendar was always celebrated as a feast and recently her celebration in the Roman Calendar has been raised also to the status of a feast by Pope Francis, in recognition of her primary role as witness to the

---

7. See José A. Pagola, *The Way Opened Up by Jesus: A Commentary on the Gospel of Matthew*, trans. M. Wilde (Miami: Convivium Press, 2012): '... celebrating Easter means understanding life in a different way. It means joyfully sensing that the Risen One is there, in the midst of our poor things, forever upholding the moments of goodness and beauty that flower within us as a foretaste of the infinite, even if the moments pass without reaching their fullness' (245).
8. See John Paul II, *Mulieris Dignitatem*, no. 16.
9. Rabanus Maurus, *De vita beatae Mariae Magdalene*, XXVII.
10. Thomas Aquinas, *In Ioannem Evangelistam Expositio*, c. XX, L. III, 6.

Resurrection.[11] Linked to her in Matthew is the 'other Mary'. Mark names the women with Mary of Magdala as Mary, the mother of James and Salome. Luke also mentions Mary the mother of James. John only has Mary of Magdala at the tomb, but mentions Mary the wife of Clopas at the Cross with Mary of Nazareth.

It is fascinating to disentangle all the Marys of the Gospels. 'Miriam' was such a common name at the time that it is easy to see how they would have become confused.[12] As the role of women was preached about in the church down the ages there was a tendency to telescope all these Marys together and to stereotype them in relation to Jesus, either as the all-pure Mary of Nazareth or as Mary of Magdala, considered as the sinful woman. But we need to reclaim each Mary for herself and see each one relating to Jesus during his life, each in her own way, and being ready again to take up the threads of that relationship in a new way in their dawning experience of his Resurrection.

Encounter

So the women turn from the emptiness of the tomb at the word of the angel, 'He has risen from the dead', and are filled with 'awe and great joy'. (28:7-8) That same dawning joy is mentioned again when, turning, they encounter Jesus who says to them: 'Joy to you'. (28:9) The more usual translation of the phrase is 'Greetings'. But understanding the phrase as Jesus bringing joy to the women, I think, brings out the essence of the encounter, as their dawning understanding of what has happened turns an ordinary salutation into one calling for a response of extraordinary joy.

Jesus is the one who seeks them out to give them a reassuring

11. See http://www.vatican.va/roman_curia/congregations/ccdds/documents/articolo-roche-maddalena_en.pdf
12. See E. Moltmann-Wendel, *The Women Around Jesus*, trans. J. Bowden (London: SCM, 1982), 61-130.

message. 'They cling to him but they need not fear; they will never lose him again.'[13] Falling down, they worship him. (28:9) Matthew is clearly telling the early Christians that worship is the proper response to the encounter with the Risen Lord. Indeed, throughout his Gospel we find a procession of people who fall down and worship Jesus: from the Magi (2:2, 8, 11), to the leper who was healed (8:2), the leader of the synagogue (9:18), the disciples in the boat (14:33), the Canaanite woman (15:25), and the mother of the sons of Zebedee (20:20). The women at the tomb are, then, the last in a long line of those who worship the Lord. What is noticeable is the diversity of those mentioned, from the foreigners who come at the birth, through those who were healed, leaders of the people and the disciples themselves, reflecting the diversity of Matthew's own community.

> Resurrection includes the whole human person and not only a part of her or him. It encompasses everything that makes a person: her joys and sorrows, his happiness and sadness, everything she has worked through in her life, and everything he has suffered, what she has accomplished and what was given him, the great things she thought and the little things he did in daily fidelity... in short the whole history of a person's life.
>
> GERHARD LOHFINK
> *Is This All There Is?*

It is interesting that the words Jesus himself says to the women echo what the angel had said: both admonish them not to fear and both insist on their telling the disciples that they are to go to Galilee where they will encounter the Lord. Matthew speaks of the disciples as Jesus' 'brothers' (28:10). In spite of their desertion, cowardice, betrayal, loss of faith and hope they are still his 'brothers', a wonderful message for the women to deliver to them. Earlier in his Gospel Matthew cites Jesus as saying, 'whoever

13. William Yeomans, *The Gospel of Matthew: A Spiritual Commentary* (Dublin: Dominican Publications, 1993), 200.

does the will of my Father in heaven is my brother and sister and mother'. (12:46-50) The fact of the Resurrection calls us all into a familial relationship with God and with one another. The will of God for Matthew is not the will of a distant and unreachable God but one who is Emmanuel, 'God with us'.

The encounter in Galilee will be detailed later in the chapter, bringing full circle, the promise of the birth chapters that Emmanuel would be 'with you always to the end of the ages'. (28:20) Galilee for Matthew is the place where the mission of the disciples would begin, whereas for Luke everything starts from Jerusalem. As 'Galilee of the Gentiles' it would be the starting point of their new mission to bring the message of Jesus to Jew and Gentile alike. Galilee had been the place where the disciples had first met Jesus and followed him.

So they, in fact, are to return home in order to meet the Risen Lord again and follow him anew. We, too, don't have to go far to meet him. We find him already where we live and from there we can bring him to others, as the early disciples did when they set out from Galilee to bring his healing and reconciling message wherever they would go, knowing that the Risen Lord was with them every step of the way.

The Day of Resurrection in Matthew's Gospel, then, is not just the dawning of another day, another week in the lives of the followers of Jesus, but the vibrant springboard that would propel them to proclaim the Risen One to the ends of the earth and calls on each of us today to do the same.[14]

---

14. Tom Wright, *Matthew for Everyone* 2, London: SPCK, 2002, 196-200.

Gospel, Year A • Matthew 28:1-10

Questions for Reflection or Discussion

As you reflect on this text, how do you think the women were changed by their meeting with the angel?

Jesus sent the women to tell the disciples that they would encounter him in Galilee. Where do you encounter the risen Jesus?

10

The Open Tomb and the Well-spring of Life

Gospel, Year B • Mark 16:1-7

LUKE MACNAMARA, O.S.B.

Introduction

The Gospel for the Easter Vigil in Year B which comes from Mark, disappointingly, contains no appearance of the Risen Lord. The anticipation built up progressively through the series of readings at the Vigil is in a very real sense left unfulfilled. The Lord's absence is puzzling indeed and invites further exploration. Attention to the characters and the context, and in particular allusions to the Old Testament, will help to unpack the richness of the open tomb. Through the ages, Christians have discovered characters and events which prefigure Jesus and his saving action. Already St Paul views the rock which provided water in the desert as Christ, and the crossing of the Red Sea as a prefiguration or type of Baptism (1 Cor 10:1-4) while the Gospel of John views the raising of the serpent on the standard in response to the plague as a prefiguration of the raising up of Jesus on the Cross. (John 3:14) This typological exegesis is also practiced by the liturgy which draws on many figures from the Old Testament.

The Gospel account opens with the mention that the Sabbath is over. For the Jews, a day begins at sunset and ends on the following day at sunset. When Jesus dies on Friday at 3.00 pm (Mark 15:34) and is buried before sundown, although only a few hours have passed, at sunset a new day begins. The Sabbath runs from sunset on Friday through to sunset on Saturday, and it is counted as a second day. Now that the Sabbath is over, the first day of the week (Sunday) has begun or the third day since the death of Jesus. Therefore, the time of the Gospel connects with the time of the Vigil. Furthermore, the timing recalls the three prophecies that Jesus made on his journey to Jerusalem about his Passion and death, and, after three days, his Resurrection (8:31; 9:31; 10:34). The first two elements of these prophecies, namely the Passion and death, have been fulfilled, and now that the third day has arrived, there is eager anticipation of fulfilment of the final element, namely the Resurrection.

The Three Women

The mention of three women, Mary Magdalene, Mary the mother of James, and Salome, recall the events of Good Friday. Even if they observed from a distance, these three women were present at Jesus' death on the Cross. (15:40) At that time the storyteller recalls that the three had provided for Jesus and had followed him in Galilee. They and many other women had accompanied Jesus in his journey to Jerusalem. The three women are thus longstanding disciples of Jesus (15:41) but it is only at this late stage in the Gospel story that this information is revealed. The male disciples whose time with Jesus has been recounted throughout the Gospel abandoned him at his arrest in the garden, apart from Peter who followed from a distance into the courtyard of the High Priest's house. (14:54)

By contrast, these women, while observing from a distance, have remained with him to the end. (15:40) Furthermore, Mary Magdalene and the other Mary demonstrate their continued faithfulness to Jesus by waiting to see what the authorities will do with his body and they later observe where Jesus was buried.

(15:47) Although the Sabbath has passed, the presence of the three women links back to the events of Good Friday where they last appeared.

The three women respect the Sabbath rest and go out only after sundown to procure scented oil or spices for the body of Jesus. It is highly unusual to go out after dark to buy anything, and their doing so is a measure of their attachment to Jesus. There is great attention given to the timing of when the women go to the tomb. After their purchase, they go home and set out only very early in the morning on the first day of the week (Sunday) when the sun had risen. It is already obvious that Sunday has begun from the evening before. The express mention draws attention to this particular day. That it is very early in the morning usually indicates somewhere between 3.00 and 4.00 am, quite some time before sunrise. However, the verse goes on to say that the sun has already risen.

The regular sequence of night and day established at the creation, as told in the First Reading of the Vigil from Genesis, is now interrupted. The in-breaking of the light into the night had been predicted by the prophet Isaiah, 'your sun will no longer set ... the Lord will be your everlasting light'; (Isa 62:19-20) and the prophet Zechariah, 'there shall be continuous day ... at the coming of the Lord'. (Zech 14:7, 9) This dawn which breaks into the night signals the coming of the Lord to save the world. This night is suffused with light.

The Easter Vigil begins in darkness, but in the middle of the night the Paschal Candle is lit, and the deacon holds it aloft three times and proclaims, 'The Light of Christ', while the assembly responds, 'Thanks be to God'. The call of Isaiah, 'Arise, shine; for your light has come, and the glory of the Lord has risen upon you', (Isa 60:1) is heard again, only the light is identified as that of Christ. This is a wonderful moment when the light of the Paschal

Candle is passed from one candle to another, till a bright glow emanates from the assembly. The irruption of Christ's dawn in the middle of the night takes place within and illuminates the entire congregation.

The Open Tomb

Since it is now the third day since Jesus' death, it is likely that his body is in an advanced state of decomposition, especially given Jerusalem's Middle Eastern climate. The visit of the women with their scented oils at this late stage (enforced by the Sabbath rest) can be of no practical use to a decomposed corpse. The anointing may be a sign of confusion in grief, a further measure of ongoing devotion to Jesus or even a hint of hope that all is not lost. Readers of the Gospel recall that Jesus had already been lavishly anointed by the woman in Simon the leper's home. (14:3-9) When some criticise the woman for this extravagant waste, 300 denarii, about a year's wages for the average person, Jesus interprets her action: 'She has anointed my body beforehand for its burial.' (14:8) Jesus doesn't require a second burial anointing. His body has already been anointed – albeit before he died. Time's normal flow has been disturbed.

Mary Magdalene and the other Mary had observed Jesus' body being wrapped in a linen cloth and being placed in the tomb hewn out of rock, and then being sealed with a stone. (15:46-47) They know where to find the tomb and the circumstances of the burial. The reported conversation of the women on their way to the tomb confirms this: 'They had been saying to one another, "Who will roll away the stone for us from the entrance to the tomb?"' (16:3) Despite the anticipated difficulty in entering the tomb, they journey in hope rather than resorting to seeking outside help to open the tomb. The inanimate stone is a fitting symbol for the finality of death. There is nothing as lifeless as a stone. However, those at the Vigil may recall the Lord's words of promise spoken through the prophet Ezekiel: 'I shall give you a new heart and put a new spirit in you; I shall remove the heart of stone from your bodies and give you a heart of flesh instead.' (Ezek 36:26) Even from stones, the Lord may draw life.

The stone blocking the entrance of the tomb recalls another stone which blocked the mouth of a well in the story of the meeting of Jacob and Rachel. (Gen 29:1-10) Just as the stone of the well is great, so is that of the tomb. Rachel comes to water her flock and cannot possibly roll back the great stone to give them water. The question of Mary Magdalene and the other women is also hers: 'Who will roll back the stone?' Jacob goes up and rolls back the stone and provides the water for the flock. Rachel rejoices at being able to water her flock. While the women were going to the tomb, they shared Rachel's doubts about rolling back the stone, but when they arrive within sight of the tomb they look and observe that the stone has already been rolled back, despite its great size. The inanimate stone, symbol of death, no longer seals the tomb. While often the tomb is described as empty, it is first and foremost a sealed tomb, which is now open. The gates of death have been thrown open. Perhaps instead of being called the 'empty tomb', it should be called the 'open tomb'.

Jacob's story is at a crossroads at this well. He has just fled for his life from his brother Esau (Gen 27:41-45), and yet the encounter with Rachel holds out great promise. The water of the deep well symbolises both danger and new life, as so often in the Bible. Perhaps the most obvious reminder of the double symbolism of water is in the account of the crossing of the Red Sea, the Third Reading at the Vigil, which brings life to the Israelites and death to their persecutors. (Exod 14-15) While the Seventh Reading from Ezekiel speaks of water giving new life (Ezek 36:16-28) the link with death is present in salvation history from the destructive flood in the time of Noah onwards. (Gen 6-9) However, God has control of the waters and tramples the waves of the oceans. (Job 9:8) Jesus, too, demonstrates this control when he walks on the Sea of Galilee. (6:47-51)

The finality of death is broken through the opening of the tomb. Jesus comes through the waters of death. Jacob's well prefigures the font of Baptism, which through the death and Resurrection of a descendant of Jacob – Jesus – has been opened once and for all. The streams of living water are now released for humankind. The *Rite of Christian Initiation of Adults* stipulates that 'the Easter Vigil should be regarded as the proper time for the sacraments of initiation'. (no. 8) The opening of the tomb opens the font for those to be baptised. In ancient baptismal practice, those chosen for Baptism, the elect, entered into the water and were submerged three times before coming out of the water. Jesus has journeyed through the waters and opened the seal of stony death for all who are baptised in him. The elect about to be baptised rejoice at this opening. This is indeed an opportune time for Baptism, when the font is freshly opened. The Vigil is also a time for all the baptised at the Vigil to rejoice in the gift of their Baptism, which they recall as they renew their baptismal promises.

In a White Robe

The women enter the open tomb. Equipped with their oils and ointments, they expect to find the body of Jesus. Instead they see a young man in a white robe seated on the right. (16:5) There is no body in the open tomb, but it is not empty. This is the second time that a young man appears in Mark's Gospel. The first appeared at Jesus' arrest in the garden. (14:50-52) While the flight of the all the other disciples is briefly recounted, special note is taken of the young man. He is wearing only a linen garment (in Greek, *sindôn,* the very word that will be used for the shroud, in which Jesus will be buried) and when those arresting Jesus take hold of it, he leaves it behind and runs off naked. The extent of the abandonment of Jesus by the disciples is epitomised in the episode of the young man. At this stage it seems as if the story of Jesus and their story is ended.

Interestingly, a similarly named linen garment was used to wrap Jesus' body at his burial. (15:46) The young man who was previously wrapped in a garment which served as a burial shroud is now wrapped in a *stolê*, a long flowing robe, such as might be worn for show by the scribes. (14:38) This high-status clothing is a garment for the living rather than a shroud for the dead.

The white colour has only been seen with the clothes of Jesus at his glorious Transfiguration. (9:3) The whiteness was of a quality that no fuller on earth could reproduce. The young man's robe shares this glorious white quality. This is confirmed by the astonishment of the three women (16:5-6) which echoes that of the three disciples at the Transfiguration. (9:6) The anticipated glory of Jesus' Resurrection beheld at the Transfiguration is now shared by them.

While, on the one hand, Jesus, wrapped in his burial shroud, has taken upon himself the shame of the flight of the young man in his death, on the other, in the tomb, the place of Jesus' Resurrection, the young man is clothed with the garment of glory. In

> White robes were given to you as a sign that you were putting off the covering of sins, and putting on the chaste veil of innocence.… And the daughters of Jerusalem beholding these garments say in amazement: 'Who is this that comes up made white?' … But Christ, beholding his Church, for whom he himself had put on filthy garments, now clothed in white raiment, seeing, that is, a soul pure and washed in the bath of regeneration, says: 'Behold, you are fair, my love, behold you are fair, your eyes are like a dove's', in the likeness of which the Holy Spirit descended from heaven.
>
> ST AMBROSE, *De mysteriis*

the early Church, the baptised would undress and be submerged in the font and then be clothed in a white robe. The exchange of everyday clothes for the clothing of immortality was more evident. This new clothing changed the status of all the baptised, since in the Roman Empire only Roman citizens, free adult males, were entitled to wear white robes. The change wrought by the Resurrection undoes all notions of hierarchy. In Baptism, the white garment is bestowed on all, male and female, Jew and Gentile, slave and free.

The young man is sitting to the right, but it is not clear what is the reference point. The positions closest to Jesus are favoured ones. They had been sought by James and John, to the annoyance of the other disciples, but these positions are reserved and not even Jesus can designate who sits there. (10:35-40) This is an implicit reference that it is God alone who decides who sits where in the kingdom.

Of the two positions requested by the sons of Zebedee, the right-hand position is the more favoured one. This is the position indicated by Psalm 110:1 and quoted by Jesus when teaching in the temple. (12:36) Indeed, Jesus promises the chief priests that they will see the Son of Man seated at the right of the Power – *i.e.*, God. (14:62) The privileged seated position of the man on the right, shared with Jesus, indicates his proximity to God's power, and that the power of God has been at work in the tomb. The young man who abandoned Jesus and ran off naked is now gloriously clothed and seated on the right.

He Has Risen

From his position of status and authority, the young man, recognising the women's amazement, first tells them to not be alarmed. He knows that they are seeking Jesus the Nazarene, who was crucified. (16:6) In this short sentence he sums up Jesus' entire journey and mission, from his origins in Nazareth to the Cross. Jesus' very first appearance in the Gospel is at Nazareth, from where he goes to the Jordan to be baptised. (1:9) The mention of Nazareth recalls his early ministry in and around Galilee until he sets out on his journey to Jerusalem. (8:27)

The women who came to the tomb have been with him since Galilee and were also present at the Cross. (15:40-42) They are the only disciples of Jesus who can testify to all that the young man has said. They are, therefore, the best placed to hear the news which follows: 'He has risen'. He is *not* where he had been placed by those who would seek to contain him. To cite Donald Juel, 'Jesus is out of the tomb, on the loose'.[1]

The verb *egeirô* (to rise) is in a passive form and more literally might be translated, 'he has been raised', which is the translation used in the NRSV. This more clearly hints at the action of God in the Resurrection of Jesus. It is also interesting that a different verb is used by Jesus, namely *anistêmi*, when speaking of his future Resurrection, after the Transfiguration and in the three prophecies of the Passion. In contrast, the verb *egeirô*, which occurs frequently in Mark's Gospel is most often employed by Jesus in his healings: Simon's mother-in-law; (1:31) the paralytic; (2:9-12); the man with the withered hand; (3:3) Jairus' daughter; (5:41) the boy with the unclean spirit; (9:27) and Bartimaeus. (10:49) The proclamation of Jesus' Resurrection with this verb connects with the return to health and life of so many characters in the Gospel. Jesus in his ministry dispenses the power of his Resurrection liberally and widely.

The elect, those to be baptised at the Vigil, also draw from this power. The many figures of the Gospel, young and old, male and female, rich and poor reflect the diversity of those baptised

1. Donald. H. Juel, 'A Disquieting Silence' in *A Master of Surprise. Mark Interpreted* (Minneapolis: Fortress, 1994), 113.

throughout the world at the Vigil. The power of the proclamation becomes a reality in their lives, as they rise up with Jesus and are clothed in white, the glorious colour of the raised.

A Proclamation of Hope

The young man continues: 'He is not here. See, here is the place where they laid him.' (16:6) The young man shows to the women that their search for Jesus in the tomb is pointless. Some of them may have witnessed Jesus' burial in the tomb, and this is confirmed by the young man when he points to where his body once lay, but Jesus is no longer in the tomb. However, he is not wholly absent because the young man seated on the right in glorious white apparel proclaims Jesus' Resurrection. From the tomb, the place of the dead, the Resurrection is proclaimed, giving firm hope to all who have died and all who face death.

There are no better people among Jesus' disciples to have come to the tomb and to have heard this proclamation than Mary Magdalene and the other women. They have witnessed not only to his ministry but also to his death and now the first announcement of his Resurrection. Only they can provide a complete witness to Jesus. These fully qualified witnesses are now commissioned by the young man to go and share the news with the despondent disciples who have abandoned Jesus, and in particular to Peter.

The special emphasis on Peter recalls his leading position as one of the first disciples to be called; (1:16-18) as the first to be selected of the twelve; (3:16) as one of the three disciples closest to Jesus who accompany him at the raising of Jairus' daughter; (5:37) at the Transfiguration; (9:2-8) and as the one who first proclaims Jesus as Messiah. (8:29) However, in his most recent appearance in the Gospel story, while Jesus bravely affirms his identity before the High Priest and Sanhedrin, Peter outside in the courtyard denies Jesus three times to a servant girl and some bystanders. (14:66-72)

Peter – with characteristic lack of self-knowledge – had promised that even if all deserted, he would remain faithful, (14:29) and when Jesus predicted that he would deny him, (14:30) he persisted, saying that he was ready to die with Jesus. (14:31) When the cock crowed for the second time, Peter remembered Jesus' word and he broke down and wept. (14:72) The special mention of Peter by the young man is thus especially poignant. The news of the Resurrection is to be especially shared with him. While the young man says nothing of Peter's failings, the hearers of the Gospel will not have forgotten them.

This too is part of the Good News, not only that Jesus has been raised, but that the consequences of his Resurrection include the forgiveness of sins. Along with the other disciples, Peter is called yet again to get behind Jesus (see 1:17 and 8:38) and follow him into 'Galilee'. The hearers cannot help but sense that Galilee may be less of a geographical location and more of a point of setting off anew, where one learns to follow Jesus again. Galilee is the place where, much to the shock of those who know how God acts, forgiveness and healing is offered to those who come to Jesus out of a conviction that in him is power. (see 2:5, and also 5:34 and 10:52)

Conclusion

The proclamation to the women ('He has risen') is not to be repeated to the disciples. Instead, the women are to say that, 'he is going before you to Galilee; it is there you will see him, just as he told you'. (16:7) This recalls an earlier promise of Jesus that after his Resurrection he would go before them to Galilee. (14:28) Remembrance is a key element in reception of the Easter proclamation. The proclamation refers to Jesus who lived and ministered among the disciples and was then crucified and buried. It is this same Jesus who is now risen.

The reference to Galilee recalls the full ministry of Jesus, the time shared with him from the beginning. The disciples are invited, on receiving this proclamation, to retrace their steps back to Galilee, to journey once again with Jesus, whom they now recognise as their Risen Lord. Galilee is not only the place of the beginning of their relationship with Jesus, it is also home to the disciples. They are not asked to visit the tomb in Jerusalem but to go and meet Jesus in their home region. It is there that he will once more lead the way, and it is there that they will see him.

The women have been *looking* a lot in this Gospel passage: they look and observe the open tomb; (16:4) they see the young man; (16:5) and they are commanded to look at the place where his body lay. (16:6) The women eventually discover where they will see Jesus, in Galilee, which is also their homeland, and where they too first met him.

> Come from that scene, O women, bearers of good tidings, and say to Zion: 'Receive from us the glad tidings of joy of the Resurrection of Christ.' Exult, rejoice and be glad, O Jerusalem, beholding Christ the King as a Bridegroom come forth from the tomb.... The Passover of delight, the Passover of the Lord, the Passover, the all-venerable Passover has dawned upon us, the Passover on which let us embrace one another with joy! O Passover, ransom from sorrow! For today Christ shone forth from the tomb as from a bridal chamber and filled the women with joy, saying: 'Tell the Apostles.'
>
> BYZANTINE PASCHAL STICHERA

The conclusion of this Gospel passage points back to the beginning. The task for contemporary disciples is similar to that of the disciples in the story. Remembering the words of Jesus, they welcome the proclamation from the tomb that Jesus is risen. The tomb is not empty. The proclamation of the young man renders the Risen Jesus present to the women, as the proclamation of the Risen Jesus at the Vigil renders him present to the congregation.

It is not enough to hear the proclamation. All contemporary disciples, even if they have abandoned or denied Jesus at times, as the disciples of the Gospel story, are invited to return to their beginnings with Jesus and to make once again the journey from their 'Galilee', their own homeland. This journey is made with the one who has died and is now risen. The journey to Jerusalem and to the tomb is no longer the same for any disciple of Jesus. This wonderful change, brought about through Baptism, is celebrated at the Easter Vigil.

Questions for Reflection or Discussion

The open tomb from which the stone has been rolled away is a sign that Jesus is not confined or restricted by death. What barriers or obstacles exist in your life that prevent you from living fully in the light of the Resurrection and how can the reality of the open tomb help you deal with them?

At Baptism, all of us were clothed in white, the glorious colour of those who have been raised. In what ways and to what extent are you aware of sharing in Christ's resurrected life?

11

Witnesses of the Resurreciton

Gospel, Year C • Luke 24:1-12

THOMAS ESPOSITO, O.CIST.

Introduction

The centre of all time is Christ, whose arms extended on the Cross embrace past, present, and future and gather them into his pierced heart. The blood and water flowing from his side (John 19:34) are channelled to us in the sacraments, most notably Baptism and the Eucharist. These sources of grace remind us that Jesus does not regard his own salvific work as something independent of us, a gift that we receive passively; rather, he desires that we share in his dying so that we may enjoy his divine life, both now and beyond the bounds of our mortal existence.

Our Catholic liturgy creates a beautiful space in which past, present, and future are again united in our celebration of Christ's life and love. The prayer over the Paschal Candle, recited at the beginning of the Easter Vigil, announces: 'Christ yesterday and today, the Beginning and the End, the Alpha and the Omega; all time belongs to him'. The Vigil wondrously highlights the simultaneous linking up of the glorious deeds wrought by God throughout history, culminating in Christ's triumph over death, with our own commemoration of that singular event 2,000 years ago. The frequent refrain of the *Exsultet*, 'This is the night', allows us to join our voices with those of the Israelites saved by the waters of the Red Sea and the first apostles to see the risen Lord on Easter Sunday. All of salvation history, from creation to our own share in the light of Christ, is gracefully condensed into this most holy memorial.

The First Day of the Week

When we hear the Gospel reading for Year C at the Vigil, we receive an extraordinary gift from the first witnesses of the Resurrection. Thanks to their testimony, recorded by Luke, we go with them to the tomb, and their frightened amazement consoles us as we ponder the magnitude of Christ's mystery in our present moment. The first verse of the reading gives the setting for the Easter miracle: 'On the first day of the week, at the first sign of dawn.' (Luke 24:1) We too gather for the Vigil awaiting the first day of the week, anticipating the dawn not simply of another day, but of the Son who will not sit again in death, and who will ultimately allow us to share in his triumph over mortality.

The conquest of death, however, surely appeared to be an extinguished hope to Jesus' followers on that first Good Friday. Luke focuses his attention on a few women who had faithfully followed Jesus from Galilee all the way to Golgotha. (8:1-3; 23:49, 55). The evangelist closes his Passion narrative by recording that these women (identified in 24:10 as Mary Magdalene, Joanna, and Mary the mother of James) see the tomb and the position of the dead body of Jesus. (23:55). They return home, prepare the customary spices and ointments for burial, and then rest on the Sabbath. (23:56) Luke notes specifically that 'they were quiet' (in Greek, *hêsuchasan*), emphasising, perhaps, their interior sorrow more than their faithful observance of the third commandment, while their Lord takes his own Sabbath rest in the domain of death.

The first day of the week, for Luke, is Sunday, soon to be the cornerstone of the Church's liturgical life. Luke relates that the women return to the tomb on that first day of the week. He does not reveal their expectations or the depths of their grief; he simply writes that they bring their spices to anoint the body of their crucified Lord. Yet their presence at the tomb, prior to any knowledge of or faith in the risen Christ, becomes the foundation for the faith of all Christians from that Easter Sunday onward. When the two men dressed in dazzling garments appear to the terrified women, they focus the women's attention on their memories of Jesus: '"Remember what he told you when he was still in Galilee: that the Son of Man had to be handed over into the power of sinful men and be crucified, and rise again on the third day?" And they remembered his words.' (24:6-8)

Memory

Luke's narrative provides us with a crucial link to our Vigil celebration: the essential role of memory in the life of faith. For Israel, memory is a lifeline to God, providing historical and personal material for prayers of praise; if a person or a people faithfully remembers the mighty deeds of the Lord in the past, they can trust that the Lord will remain faithful to them in the future. The Lord commands the Israelites to 'Remember the Sabbath day, and keep it holy'. (Exod 20:8)

Memory is also at the heart of the Exodus narrative, featuring the first instructions for the Passover meal that will become the standard liturgical feast of Israel: 'This day will be a day of remembrance for you, which your future generations will celebrate with pilgrimage to the Lord; you will celebrate it as a statute forever.' (Exod 12:14). The instructions for the Passover meal dramatically highlight the identification of present and future readers with their original Israelite ancestors who actually participated in the first Passover: 'Thus, when you have entered the land that the Lord will give you as he promised, you must observe this rite. When your children ask you, "What does this rite of yours mean?" you will reply, "It is the Passover sacrifice for the Lord, who passed over the houses of the Israelites in Egypt; when he struck down the Egyptians, he delivered *our* houses."' (Exod 12:25-27)

In a beautiful part of the current Passover meal known as the Seder or *Haggadah*, contemporary Jews are aware that they themselves take part in that original deliverance from Pharaoh when they observe the Passover: 'In each generation, everyone must think of himself or herself as having personally left Egypt.'[1] One prominent American rabbi describes the Jewish understanding of memory at Passover as 'redemptive re-experience':

> The goal [of the Passover meal] is to re-member the reality of redemption: to reassemble our own world-view in accord with the *Haggadah's* progression from degradation to dignity, to reintegrate into our lives the reality of a God who hears the cry of the oppressed. The thrill of re-experiencing the redemptive moment only brings us halfway; the ultimate messianic goal of the Seder is not to transport ourselves into the redemptive moment, but to insist that the redemptive moment can be realized in our world.[2]

Jesus adopts the same language and mindset found in the book of Exodus when he celebrates the Passover with his disciples and institutes the Eucharist at the Last Supper: 'Then he took the bread, said the blessing, broke it, and gave it to them, saying, "This is my body, which will be given for you; do this in *memory* of me."' (22:19. See also 1 Cor 11:23-25) In obedience to his command, that emphasis on memory is repeated at every Eucharistic liturgy that we celebrate. In fact, the liturgy lifts us up

---

1. Shoshana Silberman, *A Family Haggadah II* (Minneapolis: Kar-Ben Publishing, 1997), 26.
2. David E. Stern, 'Remembering and Redemption', in *Rediscovering the Eucharist: Ecumenical Conversations*, ed. R. A. Kereszty (New York: Paulist Press, 2003), 7.

Gospel, Year C • Luke 24:1-12

into God's eternal present. Through the readings and the Blessed Sacrament, our time-bound remembrance, constrained by our limitations as creatures, nevertheless provides us with a glimpse of the same simultaneous 'now', the unified eternal present, in which God dwells.

The graced logic of this liturgical tradition is clear: from the Israelite homes in Egypt to our church altars today, we look back to recall what marvellous deeds God has done. In doing so, we trust that the redemptive moment achieved by God in the past will be realized also in our present and future. In this sense, memory is truly the foundation of faith. Only those who refuse to remember, or who look back merely with regret and bitterness at God's perceived weakness or absence in their lives, are without hope for the future.

For this reason, the men in brilliant garments instruct the women to remember the words Jesus spoke to them while he was ministering in Galilee. Luke asserts that the women do indeed remember what Jesus said prior to his crucifixion, but those words now need to be understood anew; they require a re-reading, or a re-membering, in light of the Resurrection. Earlier words receding into the fog of memory have a new lens through which they take on a radically fresh life, now that the promise of Resurrection has become a startling

> Know then that there is nothing more lofty, nor more powerful, nor more healthy nor more useful later on in life than some good memory, and particularly one that has been borne from childhood, from one's parents' home. Much is said to you about your education, but a beautiful, sacred memory like that, one preserved from childhood, is possibly the very best education of all. If he gathers many such memories in his life, a man is saved for all of it. And even if only one good memory remains within our hearts, then even it may serve some day for our salvation.
>
> FYODOR DOSTOEVSKY
> *The Brothers Karamazov*

reality on Easter Sunday. The fact of Jesus' risen life thus becomes the focal point allowing the Law of Moses and the prophets to be reinterpreted and re-membered as pointing to Jesus' rising from the tomb.

In the subsequent verses of Luke's Gospel, the risen Jesus will essentially teach his disciples how to read the Scriptures already written and central to Israel's self-understanding. He walks with two disciples away from Jerusalem toward Emmaus;[3] not recognizing him, Cleopas and his companion (his wife?) confess their hopeless sadness and disillusionment at Jesus' death as they depart Jerusalem on Easter Sunday, even after hearing the women's report that the tomb was empty. Rather than reveal himself then and there, Jesus chastises them for their inability to believe all that the prophets had spoken: 'Was it not necessary that the Messiah should suffer these things and then enter into his glory?' (24:25-26) Luke then summarizes the rest of their journey: 'Then beginning with Moses and all the prophets, he interpreted for them the things about him in all the Scriptures.' (24:27). Only when the walking party reaches Emmaus does Jesus manifest himself: he makes himself known to them 'in the break-

> The Spirit of truth would by no means have permitted this hesitation, wavering in human weakness, to enter the hearts of his preachers, unless their trembling anxiety and questioning delay were to establish the foundations of our faith. Consequently it was our doubts and our danger that was being considered in the apostles.... Their seeing instructed us, their hearing informed us, their touching strengthened us. Let us give thanks for the divine plan and the necessary slowness of the holy fathers. They doubted so that we need not doubt.
>
> ST LEO THE GREAT, *Sermon 73*

---

3. For further reflections on the Emmaus account and the blueprint for the Church's liturgy already evident in Luke 24, see Thomas Esposito, 'The Way from Emmaus to Us,' *Communio* 37 (2010): 129-148.

ing of the bread', a code in the Gospel and Acts of the Apostles for the Eucharist (24:30-35).

When those two disciples recognize Jesus in the breaking of bread, they rush back to Jerusalem and confirm that they have seen the Lord. Jesus then appears suddenly in the midst of the group and asserts that the Law of Moses and the prophets all testify to his suffering and Resurrection on the third day. Luke is careful to note that Jesus 'opened up their mind to understand the Scriptures'. (24:44-49). The texts that the Christians will eventually call the Old Testament now find their fulfilment, their ultimate meaning, in the life, death, and Resurrection of Jesus. The Living One brings to life the dead pages of history and animates the prophecies that had lain idle for centuries, awaiting their time to be re-membered. In other words, the Scriptures of Israel as a whole had been pointing to some new reality, had been awaiting for centuries *someone* in particular to claim them, and Jesus possesses the authority as the Messiah and the Son of God to teach us how to read those diverse texts with him as their unifying goal.

Brilliant Clothes

Naturally, this crash course in biblical interpretation is hardly relevant to the women at the tomb when they encounter the men in dazzling garments. At the initial moment of revelation, they are simply terrified! And rightly so, for they recognize that they are standing before the awesome presence of God. In many passages of the Old Testament, a brilliant light surrounding messengers bringing a sudden announcement from God manifests the glorious divine presence to mere mortals. The women are understandably frightened, and they fall to the ground, hiding their faces from the blinding radiance of the men, knowing that this manifestation of the divine could easily kill them. (24:5. See also Exod 3; 24:1-12; 33:20 and Isa 6)

The majesty of God is revealed at the empty tomb by means of the two men. Though Luke does not explicitly call them angels, they are nevertheless bearers of a divine message regarding Jesus' Resurrection. Such a theophany (technically an angelophany but given that the angels convey a divine message it is also a theophany) terrifies those privileged to witness it, because they understand perfectly well that they, weak and sinful creatures, are not worthy to stand in the presence of the Holy One. (See also Peter's reaction to Jesus in Luke 5:1-11.) Yet it also fascinates them, enkindling in them a strong desire to be drawn closer to the mystery so tantalizingly revealed by the light and the message itself.

Belief and Unbelief

In response, the women rush away from the tomb to share their experience with the eleven apostles and other followers of Jesus. (24:9). Their recounting of what they had just seen and heard, however, does not meet with immediate rejoicing and belief that Jesus is alive. Everyone treats the women's testimony as absurd nonsense, and Luke categorically states that the disciples 'did not believe them'. (24:11). Peter at least runs to the tomb and, examining the linens left there as a remnant of Christ's burial, can only marvel at what had taken place. (24:12)

All four Gospels note this initial perplexity and unwillingness on the part of the apostles to believe in the initial report of the Resurrection. The testimony of Mary Magdalene and the other women is simply too much to bear at the outset; the hopes of Jesus' followers were lacerated so thoroughly on Good Friday that the wound of his death was still raw and fresh. And yet the witness of those women present at the empty tomb, for all their fear and hesitancy in coming to understand what transpired, is the foundation of the Church's faith in the nature of Jesus and his own living relationship with us today.

At the very beginning of his Gospel, Luke acknowledges that his account depends entirely on the testimony of 'eyewitnesses and ministers of the word' who followed Jesus 'from the beginning' and who supplied him, the author, with their own experiences of Jesus' deeds and words. (1:1-4) Prominent among those eyewitnesses are the faithful women, who became the first evangelists, instructing the apostles themselves about the marvellous reality of the risen Lord. Jesus speaks of these women, together with the apostles, as 'witnesses' (in Greek, *martures*) later on Easter Sunday. (24:48), and Luke constantly accents the nature of the first Christian missionaries as witnesses to the mighty deeds of Jesus in the early chapters of Acts.[4]

These witnesses, our simple and humble ancestors in faith, shared what they saw and heard during Jesus' ministry, but they also taught those listening to them how to read the Scriptures of Israel, just as Jesus had taught them after the Resurrection.[5] Their trembling at the tomb and doubt about the risen Lord are transformed into fearlessness as they carry the Gospel message of life from its obscure origins in Galilee and Jerusalem to the farthest corners of the earth. (Acts 1:6-8)

Conclusion

One final link conjoining our celebration of Easter with that first Sunday of Christ's Resurrection remains to be highlighted. The Vigil Gospel reading ends with the announcement that Jesus is alive, but it must be noted that Jesus himself does not appear or speak in the passage. In the verses proclaimed on this holiest of nights, the women do not actually see or hear him. They will encounter the risen Lord, but at a later point in the day, in a passage that we do not read at the Easter Vigil.

4. See 1:8; 2:32; 3:15; 5:32 and 10:39.
5. See, for example, Acts 2:14-36; 3:11-26 and 8:26-40.

This fact is significant, for it sheds radiant light on our own Easter faith in this present moment of history in which we stand. Our liturgy once again puts us in the place of those first believers who became Easter messengers without having seen their Lord alive, for we find ourselves today in an entirely similar position. We rely on the testimony of others, those particular women and the first disciples, most of them dying as martyrs, literally 'witnesses' for their faith, to confirm us as we walk toward Emmaus, unsteady in our faith. While we have the assurance of Christ's triumph over death and the forces of evil, we experience now, perhaps more acutely than ever before, the burden of his apparent absence in our midst, his seeming silence in the face of our own failings as a Church and in the increasingly hostile threats to our faith from outside.

We know, however, that darkness cannot reign where Christ's risen life animates those who believe. The act of faith allows us to perceive Christ's light bathing us and our world in a joyful peace, no matter the doubts or external difficulties we may face. We must therefore re-member, calmly and constantly, the love of Christ on that first Good Friday, a timeless and all-consuming love that will awaken us to a glorious present and an eternal Easter Sunday to come.

Questions for Reflection or Discussion

If you were to try to truly live as a witness to the Resurrection, what change would that require of you?

How you can you remember and understand afresh significant moments in your own life in the light of Christ's Resurrection.